March 12, 2008

Steve,
I like you and your courage.
I expect you have the ability to have
it pay off
Phil

Customer-Driven Sales

D0861761

Phil Kline

NOSE-TO-NOSE PUBLISHING
Dimondale, Mich.

Published by   NOSE-TO-NOSE Publishing
               Dimondale, Mich.

The images appearing throughout this book are used under
license agreement of Nova Development Corporation, Dynamic
Graphics, and T/Maker Company.

DEDICATION

Customer-Driven Sales is *dedicated to my mentor,
Grady McKay, former National Sales Trainer for the
Dale Carnegie Sales Course.*

It is the book he could have written, but never did.

I wrote it for him.

Acknowledgments

I give thanks to those who believed in me and kept my confidence level high while I worked on this book. I single out three who really made a difference.

Betty Jane Minsky, author of *Gimmicks Make Money in Retailing*. Betty Jane spent many hours giving suggestions to a trainer turned author. She advised, edited, criticized, and complimented my work. Betty Jane was my expert on writing.

Dennis Custer, Executive Director, Sales & Marketing Executives of Lansing, who gave so freely of his time and was always there when I needed advice or help. He made me feel like I knew what I was doing. Denny was my in-house sales expert.

Howard Schlossberg, author of *Sports Marketing*, Blackwell Publishers, Inc., 1996. While Special Projects Editor for the American Marketing Association, Howard went out of his way to give me encouragement and direction to get my first articles published nationally.

Contents

Contents

FOREWORD

by

Grady McKay

In 1964 when I joined Dale Carnegie & Associates in New York, one of my first jobs was to help sponsors throughout the country develop *The Dale Carnegie Sales Course*. At that time I could have used a book like this one by Phil Kline. The way to develop a product is to sell it nose-to-nose. That is where the tire meets the road. Nothing happens until a salesperson sells something.

All the success I achieved in fifteen years as Sales Trainer for *The Dale Carnegie Sales Course* I owe to Dale Carnegie & Associates. I would not give their material away to anyone else then nor would I now. *Customer-Driven Sales* is not *The Dale Carnegie Sales Course*. It is an outline of a "You Centered" face-to-face sales presentation which keeps the emphasis on the prospects and not the salesperson. It allows them to buy rather than be sold.

In thirty years of training I was always happy with the job I did and the results I achieved. Much of this was accomplished by helping salespeople realize that a sale takes place in the mind of the prospect; that by keeping our eyes and ears open and our mouths shut, we can satisfy the prospect and at the same time achieve our dreams.

I like this book very much because it agrees with my philosophy that a training manual should be like a sale. Both should be short and simple without being cluttered up with other subjects. Many salespeople have "I Trouble" and most sales presentations are too long for the prospect.

The shorter the better; the simpler the better. The study of selling is not complicated. The rules are simple. We develop the skills by working on one rule at a time. Working on one simple rule for one week can benefit any salesperson, whether new or experienced.

This is the only book on selling I have ever seen that has a built in "Rule Sheet" for each chapter. Many times chapters are so jammed full of information it is difficult to carry the high point into our actual sales. The "Rule Sheet" solves that problem. It keeps the salesperson focused on the one simple rule so it is put into practice.

The author is different also, with thirty years of selling and twenty-five years as a sales trainer. A trainer is one who has earned the right to be one. This author, Phil Kline, has earned the right and has done a marvelous job in presenting the subject to salespeople.

There is a shortage of good books on selling. I never felt compelled to add to the number on the market, nor to endorse any. This book is simple, well written, and it covers the subject well. I feel honored to have the opportunity to endorse *Customer-Driven Sales*.

PREFACE

My first venture into sales was in La Mesa, California, selling mutual funds. Or at least I was supposed to do that. But most of my time was spent playing cribbage with another associate. I had passed the necessary tests and obtained the required licenses, but I did not know how to sell. I was like the teacher who was educated on "what" to teach, but never trained on "how" to teach a teenager who did not want to be taught.

True, I had learned a "canned presentation," which meant everyone got the same pitch, no matter what his or her needs were. I tried that for four months and decided selling was not my cup of tea. The real trouble was that I had been taught to do what my sales manager did, without learning the basics of selling. I would have done a lot better if I had known that my job was to solve people's problems with mutual funds. That would have fit me perfectly.

A few years later, I was cajoled into selling radio advertising. I was fortunate in that my station had the lowest rates in town, less than half of what other stations were charging. I sold very few spots, but I learned some important lessons: (1) Lowest price is not a great advantage; (2) I was not "cut out" to be a salesman.

I then applied for a job as manager of a catering company in Lansing, Michigan, as I had a degree in Hotel and Restaurant Management. One of the requirements was that I take a sales class. I agreed and got the job. A year later the president of the company reminded me of the agreement and asked why I had not yet taken the class. I told him I had been too busy. He told me to take the class immediately or I would be fired. I took it.

I learned the magic of asking questions to find out what problems people had that I could solve with catering. Upon completion of the sales class eleven weeks later, I doubled the largest month I had ever had in sales. I quit my job as manager, went into sales, and doubled my income.

A couple of lessons were learned: (1) Like everything else, selling is learned. (2) There were skills that I could learn and still be myself when selling. I had always wanted to solve people's problems rather than just sell them something. That was a first step toward what the public demands today, Customer-Driven Sales.

Another benefit I received from the sales training was that I learned the basics in steps, i.e., step one, step two, step three, etc. That way I could teach the same steps I had learned. Most of what I had learned before were techniques that someone else had used and that had worked for them.

It's almost like learning to play golf, in that there are only about five basics to learn: using the proper club is simply using the proper tool for the job; the position and pressure of the grip connect you to the tool; even weight distribution and balance allow you to hit the ball squarely; proper alignment ensures the proper flight of the ball; finally, a smooth swing gives consistency. Golf coaches can teach you to play golf or how to improve your game because they know the basics.

I can teach Customer-Driven Sales because I know the basics. I know the five steps of selling. I know the purposes of the five steps, and I know how to use them. Along with the five steps, I know how to ask questions to find a prospect's problem and help him or her solve that problem. This book can help you learn these basics and become more professional in Customer-Driven Sales.

HOW TO GET THE MOST FROM THIS BOOK

Different people use this book for different purposes:

- Some people read it just for entertainment.

- Others who are new in selling use it to learn how to sell because it is readable and practical.

- Many already in selling realize the importance of becoming proficient in Customer-Driven Sales. They like the way this interactive method is presented in a clear and concise form that can be easily adapted to their present style of selling.

- Some people want to use it to train others in Customer-Driven Sales without having to teach them the basics first.

Which of these major benefits is most important to you? If you read it for entertainment, you will find it easy to read.

New in Selling

If you are new in selling and want to learn how to sell, you are fortunate because this book deals with the basics. What you learn here will fit with just about any type of sales training you get from other sources. Read the book through and you will have gained valuable knowledge.

Then comes the important part:

- Read and learn Chapter 1 on the five steps of selling. Learn it well enough to pass a test with an "A."

- Read Chapter 2 on the attention step. Choose those attention getters that best fit your style of selling. Complete the rule sheet for attention reminder. Use the rule sheet to remind you to work on those attention getters. Use them over and over again until they become the natural thing to do. Try some attention getters that feel uncomfortable for you and you will become more confident.

- Read Chapter 3 on tying the attention and interest steps together. Learn it well enough to get another "A." If you choose to use this optional step, complete the rule sheet and practice this step until it starts feeling natural.

- Read Chapter 4 on the general interest statement. Complete the rule sheet and learn the words verbatim. Because it is general interest, it will not change as long as you are happy with it. Practice the statement until it sounds natural, and then incorporate it into your selling. If you do so, it will sound natural in your presentations. (If you want to use the optional indicator from chapter 3, plug it in between the attention and general interest steps.)

- Continue through the chapters one at a time, reading them, completing the rule sheets and incorporating the rules into your selling. This will help you develop the skills you need to become successful in Customer-Driven Sales. Do not expect to feel comfortable with this procedure right away. You will know when you get there.

- Learn the theory behind the words and then memorize the words. They will either become your words, or you will find your own words that better fit your style of selling. This method will enable you to develop a professional presentation so you can achieve results quickly. Not only will you become confident in what you say, but the theory will help you understand why it works. (Appendices 1 and 2 will help you build your personal track.)

- Practice! Practice! Practice! Learn the words so well that you can listen to your prospects without having to think about what you are going to ask or say next. If you have to think about what you are going to ask or say next, it will be impossible to listen to what your prospects say. In the beginning, it is similar to being an actor or actress. Learn your lines and be able to say them while interacting with other people. Eventually you will no longer be acting as you say them.

New to Customer-Driven Sales

If you are already proficient in selling, and wish to add the dimension of Customer-Driven Sales, you can follow the same procedure as someone new in selling (as shown above). It makes a great review, and it is fairly easy to incorporate Customer-Driven basics into your sales. You can pick and choose chapters to practice because they are individual entities complete within themselves.

Selling Something New

Occasionally, a manager would like to become more effective at recruiting, or an experienced salesperson will want to get into another type of selling. If this is the case, develop a new General Interest Statement and new Menu Tags to fit the new product. The rest of the basics are the same for any type of Customer-Driven Sales.

If you wish to teach this sales technique to someone else, do exactly what a person new in selling would do (as shown above). Then you will not only teach the words, but you will be able to back them up with skills. Your experience will come across to your students.

John Hayden, a sales representative in Davenport, Iowa, took a sales class while selling advertising for a small radio station. He had been in sales for only nine months. Competing against twenty other professional salespeople, he won a competition for best sales presentation and an award for having done the most for the other class members—both by vote of the class members.

Here is how John did it. He adapted the words in the track to fit his selling of radio space. He then memorized his track so well that he could give it verbatim, even when in front of a group. That is the presentation he gave to win the awards in the class. I used to tell John, "You may not be the greatest salesperson in the world, but you look and sound like you are." Actually when he looked and sounded great, he *was* great. Winning the awards was nice, but not the most important benefit John received from learning the track so well.

John went on to become sales manager of two radio stations and was successful training others in the same skills he developed. When he decided to leave radio, he knew he could sell anything he would like, so he went after the job he wanted in pharmaceuticals. The way he got there was by following the steps outlined here.

No matter what your present proficiency level, or for what purpose you wish to use this book, you can always use it as if you were brand new in selling. Sometimes the best learning is when we relearn what we already know.

Try it; you'll like it.

INTRODUCTION

Marriott International is the $9 billion lodging and food service empire headed by CEO Bill Marriott Jr. In an interview conducted by Gerhard Gschwandtner, publisher of *Personal Selling Power*, September 1994, Gschwandtner states, "Bill Marriott has created a service organization driven exclusively by the needs of the customer." He quotes Mr. Marriott, "Our basic philosophy is to make sure that our associates go the extra mile to take care of customers and have fun doing it."[1]

At the Sales & Marketing Executives International Marketing Convention in Norfolk, Virginia in the fall of 1994, Bill Marriott Jr. was honored as SMEI Marketing Statesman of the Year. In his talk, he told how Marriott interviewed over 700 customers for 30 minutes each to determine what they liked about their stay at Marriott and what they felt needed improvement. Mr. Marriott stated, "The more you know about the customer the better job you can do."[2] Based on the information gathered from their customers, they made customer-driven changes.

As a result of these interviews, Marriott changed their check-in and check-out procedures. They built more than 100 of a new type of hotel that provided travelers with high-quality rooms at a budget-conscious price. They changed their dining room service

[1] Gschwandtner, G. The Marriott Miracle. (1994). *Personal Selling Power* (Sept. issue), p. 25.

[2] *Ibid.*, p. 24.

1

to fit what the customers wanted. They put runners in the kitchen so the servers could remain in the dining room where they were available to the customers. They moved a lot of the cooking into the dining room to accomplish what the customers wanted. This is what *customer-driven* means.

Many other service organizations use the same type of evaluation. I have seen them used at tennis clubs, resorts, motels, hotels, restaurants, hospitals, and many businesses.

The problem is that most service organizations do not seem to take the answers as seriously as Mr. Marriott. Many only make the changes that they like. Customer-driven means making the changes that the customer wants, not just those that the organization likes.

In Customer-Driven Sales we ask some of the same questions that Marriott asked. They are not merely a list of questions to be asked, but a method of determining what the customers want so we can satisfy their needs. The idea is not new. In 1949 Frank Bettger wrote in one of the best-selling books on sales in history, *How I Raised Myself from Failure to Success in Selling*, "The most important secret of salesmanship is to find out what the other person wants, then help him find the best way to get it."[3]

When we satisfy the needs of the customer, it builds long-term relationships rather than quick sales. Strangely enough, many times when we satisfy the needs of the customer, the result is that in addition to building the long-term relationship, we get the quick sale. Sharon Gillette of Browning-Ferris Industries (BFI) says, "When you get into people's minds to help determine their problems, and what they need, they will remember you for what you have done for them."

When we are the customers and buy from salespeople, we seek out those who ask questions, listen, and pay attention to what we want; we rebel at those who try to sell us something we do not want, and we know the difference. Something happens

---

[3] *Ibid.*, p. 41.

when we become salespeople. All of a sudden we think we have to sell something to somebody.

Sales Don't Get No Respect

When my son Phil went to Lawrence Tech University, a small private college in Michigan, he said that when they received too many demerits, their punishment was to be locked up in a room with a salesman for twenty-four hours.

There is the same lack of respect for sales at many of the larger universities in the United States. Some feature a degree in purchasing but not in sales, even though there are probably one hundred salespeople to every purchasing agent. Fortunately, there are some colleges where one can major in professional selling. One of those is the University of Akron, Ohio, where they have the Fisher Institute for Professional Selling.

The lack of respect for sales is pretty much the same in the business community. My phone directory has 714 pages in the Yellow Pages section, yet there is only one listing under sales training: mine. Every business listed in those pages is in there for the same purpose, to sell something. How do those businesses train their salespeople?

Some salespeople get in-house training from their management, some get it from reading books about how somebody else did it well, and some get it from traveling seminars that come to town and fill a hotel ballroom for a day. It seems that most salespeople just try sales to find out if they are cut out for it.

Sales is a strange profession; people often try it to "see" if they like it. To be a doctor, dentist, carpenter, mechanic, computer operator, or just about anything else except a politician, you have to learn how to do it. But to be a salesperson, all that is required is to "see" if you can do it. This makes about as much sense as the guy who asked his friend if he played the violin. His friend replied, "I don't know. I never tried."

Many people have natural talents to become successful in sales. They know how to talk to people, to sell themselves, to ask questions, to read body language, and other aspects of selling. They can make a living, but if they really want to use more of their talents and become more successful, they should take some lessons.

Without any lessons, I learned how to play golf, shooting consistently in the low eighties. That was the trouble: I never became any better; I couldn't expect to make a living playing mediocre golf. We can shoot pool, play baseball, sing, or whatever we have the inclination to do. That is great as long as we do not expect to earn a living at it.

The point is this: Selling is something we can do without lessons, but if we really want to become professional and earn the income we are capable of earning, it means lessons. If you know somebody doing the same job as you, earning twice the money as you, no more intelligent than you, then that person has developed a skill that you are not using.

Stumbling Blocks to Customer-Driven Sales

What stops people from starting in sales or becoming successful in sales? One problem is that we have friends and acquaintances who line up to tell us we are crazy to try sales, or who insist we don't need more training. Usually they are people who either "tried it" and didn't make it or who never "tried it."

If you want to find out about sales, ask someone who is successful in sales. If you want to find out about Customer-Driven Sales, ask someone who has learned how to sell that way. If you want to find out about a sales course, ask someone who completed it.

Often it is difficult to get sales managers to recommend sales training to their salespeople because they may feel as if they are saying, "I can't do it all for you." However, the owners of the company will often recommend sales training because it will put money in their pockets.

What about training? I have had people ask, "Why would you ever take sales training? You are a natural salesman." I feel like asking them, "Why did you go to medical school? You are a natural doctor." "Why did you go to engineering school? You are a natural engineer." Many people do not see sales as a profession that one has to learn.

Many who seek to improve their selling skills try to do so with education rather than training. In college I heard a teacher object to the use of the word "training," as in training students. She said, "You educate people and train dogs." I believe she was half right; I would prefer to have a dog that is house trained rather than just educated.

Take Lessons

Training is putting education to work. It is doing the things we are supposed to do. The world is full of failures who have "learned how to do it" but haven't developed the proper habits to become successful. Many have heard the story of the salesman who said, "Why should I learn more, when I don't do the things I already know how to do?"

Practice is an essential part of any training. We can take piano lessons for years, but unless we develop the skill by practicing what we learn, we will never get people to listen to us play. Selling should be learned the same way we learn to play the piano: take a lesson and practice that particular skill until it becomes a good habit. Next week take another lesson and do the same thing. Practice each new skill until it feels natural and becomes habit.

Developing skills is difficult to achieve from attending a two-hour inspirational talk, from taking an all day seminar, or reading a book. The result of these is usually a couple of ideas that we intend to put into practice, or a bunch of yellow lines highlighting the most important lessons that we learned and expect to use.

If we develop good selling habits, prospects are more likely to enjoy our presentations and will be more likely to buy. If we let prospects interact in two-way communication, they are more apt to become customers who buy over and over rather than just one time. Customer-Driven Sales is a skill we can develop by taking a lesson, practicing during our regular work week, and developing those habits that will encourage prospects to become customers.

It is similar to the way you would improve your golf game. The time to improve your game is not while playing. Spend time on a driving range driving one ball after another until what you do becomes automatic. Then hit approach shots until you start developing a natural swing; follow this with chip shots and then putting. After all the practice, the improvement will become part of your game.

It is much easier to develop the skills one by one rather than simultaneously. As you develop each skill, you will find that although you work for the skills originally, from there on they work for you.

Sometimes salespeople say, "I cannot find the time to take more training." I understand that time is important. Many others have felt the same way. Yet a certain number of them have squeezed in the time. They are the successful salespeople who ended up with more time and money. They have developed the natural talents they already had into more effective selling skills.

I remember the story about the lumberjack who went to work for a logging company back when they felled trees with axes. The first day at work he felled ten trees per hour. The next day it was only eight per hour, and a day later it had dropped to six.

His boss accused him of slacking off on his work. The lumberjack swore he was working just as hard, but the problem was that his ax was getting dull. The boss asked him why he didn't sharpen the ax, and the lumberjack said, "I have been so busy cutting trees that I haven't had time to stop and sharpen it." Do it now; take the time to sharpen your selling skills.

CHAPTER 1

FIVE STEPS OF SELLING

Most of this book is on "Selling," not "Sales," just as "Flying" is related to "Flight." We can learn about flight by studying weather, aerodynamics, theory of flight and more, but we would not do well at the controls of a plane. In flying we learn to take off, bank, turn, land, and develop all the skills necessary to live a long and happy life.

Sales includes record keeping, organization, product knowledge, identifying and locating prospects, etc. But *selling is nose-to-nose meeting with prospects with the purpose of getting them to buy products or services that will solve their problems*.

Selling is a mental art. A sale takes place in the mind of the prospect. Our job in selling is a combination of leading and following the mind of the prospect to a decision favorable to both of us. We learn to approach, to persuade, to probe, to close, and all the other skills necessary to accomplish this. The purpose is not to make a quick sale, but to make the sale and gain a customer.

This book is not dedicated to all those sales ideas, techniques, and organization necessary to become successful. This book will help develop the skills of meeting face-to-face with prospects on an interactive basis, to get them to make a favorable decision.

It would be so simple if we could just explain to our prospects how our products work, and not have to sell. But we must face the facts of life in selling: We have to sell ourselves to get in front of prospects. We have to sell them on listening to us. We have to sell them on giving us the information needed to determine what problems they have that we can solve. And we have to sell them on making the decision to buy. Our job is to "sell" our products to our prospects, not to explain what they do or how they work.

The terminology of selling has not changed much over the years, although some gobbledygook has crept in. Some authors have taken liberties with the terminology of selling, and use the buzzword of the week. This book will take the liberty of sticking to common terminology currently used in selling. That language is quite simple.

In the interest of simplicity, the word "product" will include services. Generally customers buy products and clients utilize services. In most instances the word "prospect" will be used to refer to both customers and clients.

The Basics of Selling Have Not Changed

Percy Whiting's *The 5 Great Rules of Selling* (McGraw-Hill, 1976) laid out these simple steps for successful selling: **Attention, Interest, Conviction, Desire, Close**. I once attended a course that had four basic steps. It combined **Attention** and **Interest** into the **Approach**, and **Conviction** was called **Demonstration**. Another book lists the same five steps as Percy Whiting, but puts **Desire** before **Conviction**. Some books call the **Close** the **Action Step**, but I never hear salespeople refer to the **Action**. They refer to the **Close**. No matter what book we read or what course we take, the basics are generally the same: **Attention, Interest, Desire, Conviction, Close**. Basics are still basics.

1. **Attention**: A prospect is someone who has a need, has the ability to buy, and is "willing to listen." Before our prospects will listen, we must have their Attention focused on us. If our prospects' Attention is on something or someone else, they will not listen. The best way to get their Attention, according to Whiting, is to talk about something in which they are interested, or to get them to talk about something in which they are interested. If we do so, an added benefit is that they will like us better.

2. **Interest**: We may get the prospects' Attention by talking about something in which they are interested, but we cannot keep them listening unless they feel something is in it for them. The best way to achieve this is to tell them we can do something for them that they either want or need.

3. **Desire**: Trainers say to sell the "sizzle" rather than the steak. The purpose of the Desire step is to "Sell the Sizzle." Just because something is good for prospects, and worth the money, does not mean they will buy it. They have to want it. The best way to build desire is by finding their Dominant Buying Motive.

4. **Conviction**: Even though prospects have the desire to own a product, we may still have to convince them our product is right for them; that the product will do what we say it will do; and that it is worth the price. To do this we use facts and benefits. We may also use evidence to prove what we say is true. After all, people do not believe everything a salesperson says.

5. **Close**: The purpose of the Close is not to get people to buy a product, but to get them to take favorable action, action that is favorable to both salesperson and buyer. Many times the action they take is to buy it from us and to buy it now. Sometimes the action is to take the next step that will lead to a sale. There are no magic closes, just some closing skills that work like magic.

As you go through this book, again and again you will be referred to the five steps of selling. Those five steps are the basics of selling. They form the basics for a theory of selling that pertains to all forms of selling, whether one on one, as in a sale, as a speaker talking to a group, regardless of the subject, or just in trying to get someone else to do what it is you want them to do.

The five steps are the theory, the necessary background information that allows salespeople in any form of sales to build their own presentations. One of the big problems in sales is that many who know the theory do not know how to put it into practice. Two ways to put the steps into practice are through a canned presentation or through a Customer-Driven Track.

Canned Presentation Versus Customer-Driven Track

Imagine that your physician has called to suggest you have a physical. You agree and set an appointment. You meet with your doctor, and before he takes your temperature, checks your weight, or asks any questions about how you feel, he starts telling you the many advantages of having an appendectomy. You listen as he tries to convince you that he can do a better job of removing your appendix than any other doctor in town; that he performs the service for a reasonable price; and that you will be happier without the useless thing anyway.

Then he asks for the order by trying to get you to agree to a date to get rid of this "problem" you have. Does this sound like selling? Well, this is very similar to the way many products are sold. This is called a "canned presentation." It is *product-driven.*

Without knowing your present situation or asking questions to discover your needs, salespeople who use a canned presentation tell you they have a "better product at a better price" and how happy you will be with their encyclopedias, vacuum cleaners, knives, life insurance, or whatever else they may be peddling. Everyone gets exactly the same presentation, regardless of whether or not they need the product.

On the other hand, let us say you change doctors and agree to set an appointment for a physical. This doctor uses a "Customer-Driven Track." You meet the doctor and she thanks **you** for coming in, engages in some preliminary pleasantries, and makes **you** feel comfortable. Then the doctor compliments **you** on having the wisdom to have a checkup (**Attention Step**) because it may enable **you** to solve any short-term problems **you** may have, so **you** can live a happier and longer life (**Interest Step**). Then the doctor says, "In order to determine what problems **you** may have and to conserve **your** time, may I ask **you** some questions?" Here the presentation becomes interactive.

Obviously you say, "Yes." She asks about **your** work, **your** home life, **your** age, **your** exercise programs, and a few other nonthreatening questions. You get a chance to answer the fact-finding questions and to let her know about your feelings. Then she does a few tests on **you**. This is a Customer-Driven Track. It starts with the same basic pattern for everyone, just like a canned presentation. Then it gets information from **you** to find out what problems **you** may have, rather than just trying to sell you something.

Doctors are part problem solvers and part salespeople. After determining your problem and the benefits you will achieve by solving the problem, then the salesperson part builds your desire to solve the problem (**Desire Step**).

Doctors should tell you the facts about the solution: the benefits you will gain and the cost (**Conviction Step**). Then they should ask you to do something about the problem, usually by giving options from which you can choose (**Close**).

The purposes of the doctor's Customer-Driven Track are to

motivate you to go through the questioning process, to determine what problems **you** may have, to inform **you** how to solve those problems, and to get **you** to make a favorable decision for **your** benefit (**Close**).

Our fictional doctor has used a track that has **Attention**, **Interest**, **Desire**, **Conviction**, and **Close**. This is what we do with a Customer-Driven Track in selling: tailor it to our own product, to our personality, to determine what problems our prospects have, and convince them to solve those problems.

The Customer-Driven Track

What is it? (Whatever it is, it is full of "Theys.")

The Customer-Driven Track is a series of statements and questions designed to get the prospect to: like us, listen to us, be willing to answer personal questions, and in all respects, become a model prospect. The track is designed to help prospects determine what problems **they** may have that we can solve with our product. The track is designed to have the prospects relay to us what **they** want to purchase; what benefits **they** want from the purchase; how to get **them** to desire the product; how to handle any objections **they** may have; and relay to us when **they** are ready to buy.

It is called a track because, just as a railroad track takes us from station to station, the selling track takes us step by step through the five steps of selling. If we get sidetracked at any step, we can get back on at the same place we got off. We can pass through any station, or step, without stopping. For instance, if we determine that the prospect has mentally taken some step or steps without our help, we should skip them. If during my Attention Step, for example, I found that the prospect was ready to make a decision, I would go right to the Close.

Is it used the same for everyone?

The start of the Customer-Driven Track is similar for almost everyone (just as a doctor will ask almost the same questions and do the same tests for almost every patient). From there, the track takes us to where the problems lie for that particular prospect, and on to the solutions we recommend.

When is it used?

The Customer-Driven Track is used any time we wish to discover if the prospect has a problem we could solve with our product. Or when we know the prospect has a problem we can solve, and we want the prospect to discover that. It cannot be manipulative, because in the process of going through the track, both the salesperson and the prospect make the same discovery.

How is it used?

The track is used without any stuttering or stammering. It must flow so naturally that both we and the prospect are at ease. We must know our track well enough to go through it without thinking about what we are going to say or ask next. By doing so, we can concentrate on watching and listening to the prospect. We must watch and listen, because decisions take place in the mind of the prospect. And we must be able to see or hear when those decisions are made.

A very successful sales manager I knew in Illinois hired salespeople only after they had learned his track verbatim. He would put them in a room and have them face the wall, repeating the track until they knew it word for word. When they had memorized the track, he would hire them. Those who either would not do it or could not do it would not be hired. The sales manager knew that if they would not learn the track, they would not do all the other things required to become successful salespeople. There was no sense in wasting his time or theirs. It was no accident that he managed one of the most successful branches of an international organization.

Why is it used?

For a new salesperson, a Customer-Driven Track gives confidence because it flows smoothly. It brings success earlier because the salesperson knows what to say. Most new salespeople are nervous, as they fear saying the wrong thing, or fear not being able to answer a question. A salesperson's confidence is transmitted to the prospect, causing them both to feel more comfortable and make the sales process easier.

For the experienced salesperson, a track puts the sales presentation in order. Brad Wright of Century Cellunet says, "By reading many books and listening to many tapes I learned a lot about selling. I have retained all this information, but it was sitting there in a big basket that I had to sort through to make it usable. The track has introduced organization to this knowledge so that it is usable in logical sequence. This makes selling easier."

Most books on selling state that it is important to determine the prospect's "Dominant Buying Motive" (DBM). I have yet to read exactly how to do so, or how to know when that has been achieved. The DBM is the emotion that causes the prospect to buy *now*. How to determine that emotion is built into the track in simple terms.

Prospects can tell us what they want to buy and how to sell it to them. The track enables us to determine what benefits excite prospects and tells us how to get them to do something about it. Interestingly enough, the best information on why someone should buy now, rather than putting it off, can be obtained from the prospect.

The Customer-Driven Track is an interactive system that helps us sell the way selling should be conducted. Both the customer and the salesperson end up with more than they started with before they did business together. Not only that, but it makes selling easier and more productive.

CHAPTER 2

THE ATTENTION STEP

A farmer sold a mule to his neighbor with the promise that in order to get the mule to obey, all that had to be done was to whisper the command in the mule's ear. The neighbor tried whispering commands into the mule's ear, but the mule refused to obey and would do nothing. He took the mule back to the farmer and told him the mule would not obey, and he wanted his money back. The farmer took a fence post and smacked the mule across the back of the head and then whispered in its ear. The mule immediately obeyed. The farmer then turned to his neighbor and said, "First, you have to get his Attention."

This is how it is in selling; we don't hit the prospects with a fence post, of course, but we do have to get our prospects' Attention before we can convince them of anything.

In the Attention Step we really have two goals. One is to get the prospects to focus on us, and the other is to get them to like us. This process is sort of like going next door to borrow a tool from our neighbors. First, we may compliment them on their lawn, their home, or their children. This accomplishes both goals. It gets their minds off of what they were thinking about earlier and they like us because of the compliments.

Likewise in sales, we break the ice with a pleasurable experience. The prospect must have an open mind to which we can sell, rather than one cluttered up with thoughts of problems at home, or with the business, or what they were doing five minutes ago, or what they will be doing later. Somebody said once that it is almost as if the prospect should look up and say, "I wonder what this nice person wants?"

Most of us are familiar with a speaker starting a speech with a joke. The purpose of the joke is similar to the Attention Step in sales: to get the audience to like and focus on the speaker. However, a joke is not particularly suited to use as an Attention Step in sales. This is because some prospects do not appreciate their business thoughts being interrupted by the back-thumping, joke-telling, traveling salesman image of old.

Sometimes a joke is appropriate. John Hayden sells pharmaceuticals to doctors. Sometimes it is very difficult to get their Attention, especially when they are booked up with appointments and have people waiting. John told me that one time when he did not have the doctor's Attention, he told the doctor, "I want to tell you about the nutritional value of this drug." The doctor looked up and said, "There is no nutritional value in this drug." John said, "Yes, there is. You write prescriptions for it and my kids will eat." The doctor smiled and said, "OK. You win."

Be careful though. One of my best clients became my client after he was turned off by the jokes of his previous agent. He called me and said he did not want to deal with the other salesperson. The purpose of the Attention Step is to build a relationship, not destroy it.

Some Ways to Get a Prospect's Favorable Attention

Gifts. Fuller Brush Company made this famous by offering a small gift brush at the door before saying anything. People give calendars, bottle openers, jar or can openers, refrigerator magnets, rulers, coloring books, gift certificates, and numerous other items. The gift can be relevant to the product we are selling, but does not have to be. (Obviously the coloring book would be better geared toward a product where the users are children, and the openers or magnets would be more suited to a product for the kitchen). The gift may or may not have the company name on it, as the purpose here is not to advertise but to get the favorable Attention of the prospect.

For years when I was in the life insurance business I bought calendars for my clients, the type where appointments could be written in the squares of the dates. Women seemed to like them because they could record appointments or dates for the entire family. Not only did it keep my name in front of them in a favorable light, but I also used it as an Attention Step in talking to new clients. I gave them a calendar before I gave my name, because frankly, people were more interested in the calendar than they were in my name.

A word of warning: The gift used as an Attention Step should not be expensive. An expensive gift may make the prospect feel uneasy, which is the opposite of what we are trying to achieve. I know a salesperson who was referred to a prospect by the prospect's CPA. When he called on the new prospect he presented him with a monogrammed silk shirt. The prospect felt like he was being bought and threw the salesperson out. Then he called up the CPA and chewed him out for sending that salesperson over. Not only did the expensive gift cost the salesperson the new prospect, but he also lost the CPA as a client.

Often a gift can be used as an Attention Step because it may lead right into the Interest Step, where we get the prospect to want to hear about our product. An example is a company that sold thermostats. To gain Attention, they gave the prospect a small metal beetle with a thin strip of metal underneath. The salesperson would put the beetle in the prospect's hand, and a few seconds later, the beetle would snap and fly into the air. Then the salesperson would say that their thermostats were made of the same two metals as the beetle; they were bonded together. The small amount of heat from the prospect's hand caused the metal to flex, and the company's thermostats were just as sensitive to heat changes as the toy beetle.

Another example of the value of using gifts is related by Bob Baxter, a producer of videos for business, industry, and government. He was having trouble getting anywhere with one of his prospects. While getting some pre-approach information on him, Bob discovered that the man was a weekend sailor. When Bob met with the prospect, the first thing he did was give him a videocassette of Charlevoix, Michigan, a Great Lakes port for sailing boats. They immediately started talking about boats and sailing. Bob finally got the appointment to talk business. Bob's cost for the video was only $2.50.

Johanna Lubahn, Regional Manager for the Michigan National Bank, is in charge of training for over fifty branches. She understands the importance of constantly selling major accounts on maintaining their accounts with the bank. Because of this, she has taken sales training and knows the basics well. When a new major city was added to her territory, she made a call on the person who represented the bank's largest account in the area.

As Johanna realized the importance of making a good first impression, she gathered some information on the person who handled the account. In doing so, she discovered that the same person had handled the account for over twenty years. When she made her first call on this person, she presented her with a small daily calendar for her desk. The woman said, "Thank you, this is the first time I ever received a gift from your bank." She was not looking for a gift, but imagine handling a major account going for twenty years without someone paying attention to that fact.

An interesting method of regaining lost Attention was developed by Jim Pitchford of Re/Max Home Professionals. He says that sometimes when talking to prospective clients in their homes, a child will interrupt his presentation. When this happens, he asks permission to give the child a gift.

When approval is given, he gives the child a magnetized business card and tells the child, "This is a magnet and it is yours. Please put it on the side of the refrigerator at your eye level so you can see it." Jim says that this works every time. Not only do children like the magnet, but the parents appreciate it when Jim is able to continue with his presentation.

Startling Statement. Grady McKay was National Sales Trainer for The Dale Carnegie Sales Course. A few years ago I accompanied Grady when making cold (unannounced) calls on manufacturing firms in New Jersey. Upon getting in to see the manager of a large plant, he opened the conversation by saying, "Did you see what your secretary is doing?" The boss answered, "No. What is she doing?" Grady told him, "She is greeting visitors with a big smile on her face and a pleasing voice. It is so nice to be greeted by such a pleasant person." Grady startled the prospect and achieved the desired effect, favorable Attention.

Just like jokes, sometimes a startling statement will backfire and destroy a relationship rather than build it. On the other hand, there are times when a startling statement is a necessity. Sometimes it is necessary because a salesperson has not been successful in getting a prospect's Attention. Other times, because of circumstances, it is obvious that on the first contact something startling must be used.

Lynne VanDeventer, with Prudential Hubbell Realty in Lansing, Michigan, perennially lists and sells more homes than any other real estate agent in Michigan. She is usually among the top ten agents in the United States. Here is the story of how she got the attention of a woman who moved to Lansing when her husband was transferred there.

Lynne was told by her manager that the man was being transferred to Lansing, but his wife was very unhappy about the move. The manager told Lynne that she did not have to work with the wife if she did not wish to, adding that the home would be in the $250,000 bracket.

Lynne called the woman, who went on for about twenty minutes telling how unhappy she was about moving to Lansing, how important she was, and how, if she decided to work with Lynne, Lynne would have to do exactly what she wanted or she was not going to buy anything.

Lynne finally got a word in edgewise and shocked another agent standing nearby by saying to the woman, "It sounds like you are spoiled rotten." The woman replied, "What did you say?" Lynne repeated, "It sounds like you are spoiled rotten. You are used to having the best, and you expect the best. I know exactly what I am up against if I decide to work with you. I am going to have to drop everything else and devote my time entirely to you. I am going to have to show you only the best, because you know the difference. You know quality."

The woman replied, "Nobody ever told me that before. You are right. I am spoiled. And you know something, I like you."

Lynne told me that she sold the woman a home and became friends with her. Lynne said the woman would often tell friends in front of her, "Do you know what she called me the first time I talked to her?"

What impressed me with this story was that Lynne knew she had to get the woman's Attention, or neither of them would achieve what she wanted. In this case the salesperson got the prospect not only to focus on her, but to even vocalize the other purpose by saying, "I like you." Also the startling statement was relevant to what Lynne wanted to do for the prospect.

After I wrote an article about this Attention Step of Lynne's, I sent her a copy. Over a year later when I had lunch with her, she told me that the story gave her the idea of using something similar for her Attention Step again and again. When she meets someone who obviously dresses in good taste or drives an expensive car, she tells them something like this: "You are spoiled. Your dress, your car, and other things about you tell me that you are used to good things. I'm glad you are spoiled, and I am going to spoil you even more by doing all those things that will make buying a home enjoyable for you."

Scott Ferguson, one of my life insurance agents, was making one of his first selling calls and was working on the Attention Step. He walked into a retail store at a large mall, and as the sales clerk greeted him, Scott pointed to a counter and asked, "Did you see what just ran under there?" The clerk said, "No. What was it?" Scott then told him it was nothing, but that he was just practicing his Attention Step. Scott got away with it, but I do not recommend that type of Attention Step. It has no relevance to the sale, unless of course, you are selling mouse traps.

Demonstration. Walk through a mall, and as you come upon a music company, you may see someone playing an organ outside the store. Another store may have a closed-circuit TV that shows you on the screen. Nearby, a demonstrator is handing out little delicacies cooked in an oven in front of the store. Usually in outside selling, we do not have the opportunity to get someone's Attention with an actual product demonstration. Therefore, we must devise novel and interesting ways to get prospects to focus on us.

Dick Lorencen sold for a roadside sign company. He used to walk into a prospect's office with birthday candles that relight themselves after being blown out. After lighting one he would blow it out. It would relight itself.

Dick would then explain how this compared to his roadside signs: in effect, each time potential customers drove by the sign, it was lit up for them to see. When they passed the sign it was as if the light went out, but next time the potential customers drove past the sign, it was lit up carrying the message to be seen again. Unlike newspaper, radio, or TV, where the light disappeared after one time, the roadside sign was seen by the customer again and again.

Example. Salespeople may use an example of what others did, and how they benefited. "Joe and Mary Doaks, your neighbors down the street, had their home broken into while they were out of town last week. Nothing was taken because they had an alarm system that . . . " Here the salesperson explains that because Mr. and Mrs. Doaks were protected by one of the company's alarm systems, they were spared financial loss and the loss of many family heirlooms.

The Attention Step is the story about the neighbors down the street. It is relevant to the product because it was the product that gave the story a happy ending.

Question Bearing on a Need. Kerry Haynor is Sales Manager of Great Lakes Treatment. They sell inert chemicals that reduce lime deposits in boilers. His Attention Step: "If there were a way for you to reduce the maintenance required on your boilers and have them last longer, you would certainly want to know about that, wouldn't you?" If the prospect says, "Yes," he continues with his Interest Step. "The reason I mention that is because I feel I can show you how to reduce the maintenance required, have them last longer, and at the same time reduce your costs." That generally gets them interested.

Exhibit. As an Attention getter, an exhibit is something we can show or hand to the prospect. A former class member wrote me a letter explaining how much she gained from the sales class she took. When I make a call on a prospect who can relate to that former class member, I can get Attention by handing the letter to the prospect.

An exhibit can be a picture, a letter, a poster, or a sample. It can be anything that will get the prospects' minds off what they were thinking about and focused on what I want them to think about. Many times an exhibit, like an example, is not a particularly great tool for getting the prospects to like us. But exhibits are effective because they usually get right to the reason for our visit.

A salesperson who sold ball bearings told me about his experience with exhibits. One particular purchasing agent would do paperwork during his presentation, and as a result, never gave full Attention to the salesperson and never bought. One day the salesperson walked up to the P.A.'s desk and rolled a ball bearing across it. The P.A. caught it before it rolled off the edge and asked, "What is this for?" That was the first time the salesperson had ever gotten his Attention. He went on to tell what it was for, and got his first sale there.

Sometimes a gimmicky type of exhibit is well suited to get Attention when we have not been able to get anywhere with a prospect, or when we know we have only one shot at it. Gimmicks should not become a regular part of our presentation, because some people do not appreciate them. A basic rule in selling is only to use what is necessary to accomplish the job.

I remember a story about a computer salesperson who was having difficulty closing an order with a large firm. The buyer  would listen but would never buy. The salesperson walked into the buyer's office one day and walked straight to the window. He opened the window and threw a dollar bill out. He peeled off another and threw it out while the buyer looked on. After watching three or four dollars go floating out in the breeze, the buyer asked, "What are you doing?" The salesperson tossed another out and said, "I am throwing dollar bills away."

"Why?" asked the buyer. The salesperson answered "Why should you care? I am only throwing dollars away. Every day you go without our computer system, you are throwing away hundreds and thousands of dollars." The order was placed.

Here the Attention Step was throwing the money out the window. When the salesperson said, "Why should you care? I am only throwing dollars away. Every day you go without our computer system, you are throwing away hundreds and thousands of dollars," the salesperson was giving an Interest Step. Remember in Chapter 1, it was stated that one of the purposes of the Attention Step was to get the prospect to focus on us. The purpose of the Interest Step is to get the prospect to listen to us. Notice that in this story about the use of an exhibit, the Attention Step was non-product related but relevant to the benefit the prospect could receive from the product.

I sold to a company that had two divisions, each with its own buyer. I did well selling to one division but could never get to the buyer of the other. One day I wrote out a personal check for $1,000 to the buyer I could never reach. I gave the check to the buyer's secretary who took it to the buyer. Within two minutes the buyer was standing before me saying, "What is this for?" I said, "It is worthless, but I can do more for you than that if I can have about ten minutes with you." He gave me the ten minutes and I made my first sale there.

Furniture dealers spend a lot of money on television commercials. Char Gibbs was selling television spots in Lansing, Michigan. She was not having any luck getting in front of one large furniture dealer, so she decided not to depend on luck, but to go to a better Attention Step. On the dealer's birthday, she arrived with a cake, complete with candles. I don't remember if she made a sale, but she did get the appointment.

Exhibits can be fun and they can be effective in gaining Attention if used properly. They should not be just entertainment but should be relevant to the purpose of our selling call.

Referral. Almost without exception, salespeople say the referral is the best way to approach a prospect. Prospects are not as apt to throw us out on our ears if we are sent to them by a friend, business acquaintance, or relative of theirs. While they may see us with some reluctance, referrals do give us the opportunity to get prospects interested in what we can do for them. Using the referrer's name is the Attention Step, while telling them what we can do for them is the Interest Step.

When I trained agents in my insurance agency, I never trained them in securing prospects by any method other than referrals.

The reason was because referrals are the best prospects. The very fact that there exists a relationship between the person who gave the referral and the prospect makes the Attention Step effective. Why get prospects in any other manner if referrals are so great?

One of my agents, Russ, decided to get prospects from a list of people who obtained mortgages to purchase real estate. He used this list diligently. One day when reviewing his performance I asked him what source of leads had generated most of his business. He said the mortgage list had. I asked him for the exact figures. He checked his records and came back with the revelation that most of his leads were from the list but most of his sales were from the few referrals he obtained.

But there is a problem with obtaining referrals. Just about every salesperson knows that referrals are the best prospects; they are the easiest prospects to get, they do not cost anything, and they are easy to get appointments with. Yet salespeople do not ask for referrals due to the fear of rejection. That is why Russ decided to buy a list that was not nearly as effective as referrals that were free.

Most successful salespeople state that they have more success selling prospects obtained by referral than from any other form of prospecting. They invariably explain that other salespeople should ask for referrals as well. Big deal! Every salesperson knows that. The problem is not that they don't know they are supposed to ask for referrals, the problem is that they do not do it.

A method of solving this problem is contained in Chapter 19, Getting Warm Prospects.

Compliments. This is plural because we should compliment early and often. It seems that nowhere in the educational system are we taught to tell people what we like about them. In a class I taught, a class member decided she would work on this herself. She decided that for two weeks she would not criticize her fourteen-year-old daughter, but would compliment her instead. At the end of the two weeks she told the class what happened.

She said that on the first day, between the time her daughter came home at 4 P.M. until she went to bed at 10 P.M., she criticized her daughter ten times and did not compliment her once. I remember the woman stated that if she continued that pace for a whole year, she would have criticized her daughter 3,650 times a year—or 2,610 times if she gave her the weekends off. This mother kept working on compliments, and later in the class reported that she had managed to reduce the criticism and establish a better relationship with her daughter.

Many of us find it difficult to compliment others because we do not do so often enough to feel comfortable doing it. When we do say nice things about others, they like to be around us. When we compliment their children, their possessions, whatever they or their families have done well, they are more apt to do business with us. We should look for something we like about other people in any type of a business situation and tell them what it is we like about them. If we do this, we will never have a problem getting Attention.

I hear people say they resist paying compliments because compliments seem manipulative in a selling situation. That is like saying we should not be nice to people who come in our place of business because we are manipulating them. Usually the real problem is that we so seldom tell others what we like about them, we are out of our comfort zone when we do tell them.

Many times I have heard that salespeople have to get out of their comfort zones and do things they do not like to get the things they do like. I guess sometimes this is true, but there are many ways of getting around some of these nasty jobs rather than just bulldozing through them. There is a painless method of getting used to paying compliments.

As you watch people, think to yourself what you like about them: coworkers, friends, prospects, family, everybody. Don't tell them, but just practice in your mind. Once you get good at it, which should be in a very short time, start telling them what you think. Tell them, "I like the way you_____ because____," or "I like you because____."

When someone is going to play the piano in concert they do not do their practicing in front of an audience but in private. When they get pretty good at it, they play for their friends and/or family. After they have practiced in front of these nonthreatening people, they are ready to play in concert in public. Do the same with compliments: practice in private and later with nonthreatening friends and family. After you get good at it, then do so in a sales situation. Work your way up to it one step at a time. As Jerry Carlson from Kalamazoo, Michigan says, "Inch by inch is a cinch; yard by yard is hard."

The Prospect Furnishes an Exhibit. Sometimes there may be an article or picture hanging on the wall of a prospect's office that is so well suited to an Attention Step that it may accomplish much more than we could ever hope for. Sometimes the picture is not a picture, but "as pretty as a picture."

LaVern Rice was President of the Michigan Realtors Association. One day I went along with him when he was trying to list some expensive homes that were being built around a lake. We met the builder in back of one of the homes and walked through the garage to the front of the home facing the lake. The builder had constructed a line of rustic-style homes along a ridge covered with trees.

LaVern looked down the line and said something like, "This is beautiful. These homes fit in so well with the surrounding woods and the lake. You didn't cut down any of these beautiful trees, but built right between them, didn't you?" The builder said that he had tried to maintain the lots in the same natural state as they were in before the homes were built. LaVern asked the builder if that was his idea, and the builder said it was. LaVern even complimented the man on the work of a trim carpenter working on one of the homes.

Finally, when the builder had a chance to say something after all the compliments, he said, "Would you like to list these homes and sell them for me?" I will always remember LaVern's reply: "I would be honored to." His Attention Step made the entire sale.

Craig Benham was a realtor attending a sales class I was teaching. He made a report on how he used an Attention Step while trying to get a listing of a residence. He said that when he was invited into the woman's living room, he saw a collection of oil paintings that he liked. "Did you paint these?" he asked. She said, "Yes," and asked him to come into the next room where she had her studio and more paintings she had done. Craig got a half-hour tour, and then the woman asked him if he would sell her home for her. Once again, an Attention Step made the entire sale.

John Forsberg of Forsberg Advertising Group tells about the time he went to see a company president. John is a photographer, and while waiting in the outer office for the president, he spied a photograph on the wall that was quite unusual. The president came in a businesslike manner and directed John to another room.

Before they went into the other room, John asked the president if he could tell him about the building that was in the photograph. The president told him it was a resort down South, and he was so impressed with it that he had gone back there expressly to photograph it. He talked about the incident for a while, and on the way into the other office, he indicated that they could do business with Forsberg Advertising. John said he didn't even have to do any selling. The Attention Step did it for him.

If you see something unusual on the wall, it is probably there because someone is proud of it. But be careful because ten other salespeople may have already mentioned it. Or maybe the boss hung it there and the prospect despises it. Do not make a big deal out of it yourself, but give the prospect the opportunity to make a big deal out of it.

Years ago, my supervisor was making a cold call on the publisher of a newspaper and asked me to go along with him to see how it was done. While waiting for the publisher to come to the meeting room, my supervisor stood near the door where the publisher was due to appear. I saw a wood carving on the wall far on the other side of the room, and positioned myself facing the carving with my back to the door where the publisher was supposed to enter.

When the publisher entered the room, he swept right on by my supervisor and came over to where I was. He asked, "Do you know what that is?" I told him that I did not. He said that it was a deer spear and then said nothing else, waiting for me to ask him what it was for. I asked, "What is it for?" He told me what it was for, and we had a laugh. Then he told me how he had seen one up north and had this one made specially for that room so people like me would ask about it.

Of course, I knew that. That is the reason I stood there: to make it a pleasurable experience for our prospect. All this time my supervisor just stood watching, probably wondering what was going on because he didn't know much about Attention Steps. The call was successful because the Attention Step gave us a chance to make a presentation.

Sandy Shaw, a Realtor with Prudential Hubbell Real Estate Company, specializes in developing and selling newly constructed homes. She also has a great way of getting the Attention of people she is working with. When her prospects have little children, Sandy kneels to talk to the children, sometimes having an extended conversation with them.

Even though for a time she ignores the parents, they appreciate the attention she shows to their children, enough that it would be tough for them to buy from anyone else. I do not believe Sandy does this simply as an Attention Step; she does it because she loves children, but it is also an effective part of her sales technique.

May I Help You? "No, thank you. I am just looking." In retail selling we must make certain we never use an Attention Step to which the customer can say, "No, thank you. I am just looking." That is a dead-end street. I remember walking into an appliance store to look at a washing machine. I was thinking about buying one, but I really did not want to buy one that day.

The sales clerk came up to me and said, "You know, that machine has no belts or gears to go bad and need repair." I asked him how it worked, which is exactly what he wanted me to do. I bought that washer. If he had asked, "May I help you?" I would have said, "No, thank you. I'm just looking."

Bob Plesscher with Re/Max Home Professionals told how someone got his business because of an Attention Step. Bob was looking for a new suit when a salesperson approached him and asked, "May I help you?" Bob, of course, said, "No thanks, I'm just looking." Later, another salesperson came up to him and said, "I'd say you are about a 40 long. Gray or green would look great on you." Bob bought a gray suit from him.

Jim LaBlanc, of Denny's Schwinn, decided he needed an Attention Step for an add-on sale after he had successfully closed on an exercise bike. He decided to try to sell heart monitors for the bikes by setting off the beeper on a monitor after he had closed the sale on a bike. He then found that he sold twelve heart monitors for every sixteen bikes sold, instead of the one for every sixteen he'd sold before he decided to use another Attention Step after the first sale had been made.

When should we use the Attention Step? Should we do it before we introduce ourselves, or after? Should we have "preliminary pleasantries" first? The answer is: Whatever way we feel most comfortable, and the way that will best get rid of any barrier that may exist between salesperson and prospect in the first few moments of the approach.

Either way, we should expect to feel uncomfortable the first few times we work at getting a prospect's favorable attention. It will not be uncomfortable for the prospect, but a nice experience for him or her. As we consciously use the Attention Step, we will become more comfortable with it and more confident. Remember, prospects are always comfortable with it.

John Lehman, who sells Chevrolet trucks for Bud Kouts Chevrolet, said the most important thing he learned from his sales class was to compliment people on what they were driving when they drove up to buy a new truck. This is a turnaround because it seems that most auto or truck salespeople are scared to death to say something nice about the old one. Perhaps they are afraid they will talk prospects into keeping it.

People are attached to the cars they have driven for a few years. Some of them treat their old cars like old friends. I remember years ago I admired a little red convertible for a long time. As soon as I got a new job and I could afford it, I took my old car down and announced that I wanted to buy the convertible, and wanted to use my old car as a trade-in.

Someone came out and looked my old car over, criticizing the tires, the little rust it had, and a couple of small dings. I took my keys and left, went to another dealer, and bought a new car from them. I loved that old car; it had served me well. The guy blew the sale. He should have complimented me on the car I had bought before; it was a nice car.

I once went to look at a 38-year-old Austin Healey. I say look at it, because I really did not want to buy the first one that I looked at. It was in beautiful shape and I immediately thought, "I should maintain a poker face so this guy doesn't know how much I want this car." I went with my sales training and told him, "This is in beautiful shape. I never expected anything so nice." He told me that he had had it for fourteen years and had driven it less than 4,000 miles, but he spent many hours working on it to put it in that shape.

We talked about how nice it was and then I told him that I really did not know what it was worth, but that I would give him $1000 less than he was asking. He immediately said, "I'll split the difference with you and take $500 less." I said, "OK," and bought the car. Before I left he said that he was happy that I bought it because he knew I really appreciated the car and would take care of it.

The worst Attention Step in the world is to criticize what the prospect bought before. I remember a salesperson who was selling some sort of material for filling teeth. In class he said he asked the dentist, "Who sold you this junk?" As he was escorted out the door, he remembered he was talking to the person who had been dumb enough to buy that junk. Don't criticize, compliment.

If we have talked to the prospect before, and have used an Attention Step, when we meet that prospect again we need another Attention Step. We can either use a different one or talk about the first one. For instance, if the first time I tell my prospects the nice things someone else said about them, when I meet them again, I will show them where it was written down on my prospect card. Then we talk about the nice things again.

Why Are You Having Lunch with Me?

An interesting and effective method of getting prospects' Attention on the first face-to-face visit, after securing the appointment by phone, is to ask them, "Why are you meeting with me?" or "Why are you having lunch with me?" Invariably they will answer, "Because you asked me." Then I ask, "But why did you accept? You don't have lunch with everyone who asks you." That generally wipes their minds clear of what-

ever was there, and then I get my bonus. They will tell me what they expect to get from me, for example, "It is about time we reviewed our life insurance program," or "We have been looking at a better way of doing such and such."

Sam Walker hired a new salesperson and recommended that he take my sales class. I called the man, who agreed to meet me for breakfast. After a few pleasantries, I asked him, "Why are you having breakfast with me?" He instantly replied, "Sam told me to. I am not interested in your class but Sam wanted me to meet with you, so here I am."

I knew that his only desire at that particular time was to have breakfast and get out of there, but I just ignored his reason for being there and put him on a Customer-Driven track. As it turned out, I did not ask him to join because he already knew everything there was to know about sales.

I was happy to determine his reason for being there. It is like finding out ahead of time that you have a hostile witness in court. That is the nice part of asking this question; right away you know where you stand.

Some automobile salespeople say that they do not need an Attention Step because people have already decided to buy a car when they walk in the door. True, they may have already decided to buy a car, but what salesperson will make the commission on it? The only thing it means when someone walks in the door is that the door is not locked.

Some other salespeople say that they do not need a new Attention Step each time they return to a present customer because they have already built a relationship with that person. True, they may have a fine relationship, but the fact that they are making another call means there is something important they want to discuss. It is nice to have the customer want to discuss it also.

Sales trainers often say, "selling is a prospecting business." And prospecting is the most unpopular part of their job. If they did a better job in the Attention Step, they would not have to spend that much time finding new prospects. They would sell more to the ones they had.

Before you start selling, be sure to get the prospect to focus on you and to like you. Selling will be easier, and you will become more successful.

CHAPTER 3

TYING ATTENTION AND INTEREST TOGETHER

When my son Phil was ten years old, he was constantly losing his winter gloves. My wife finally tied the two gloves together with a long twine and ran the twine through both sleeves. That way the gloves were right there when Phil needed them but he could not accidentally lose them.

When I was in the Army, I carried a canteen for water while in the field. There was a twine that ran between canteen and cover so that the cover was there when I needed it, but I could not accidentally lose it.

The purpose of tying the two objects together was the same in both instances: not to lose one of them. There is one major difference between the situations, and this is important in selling. If my son lost his gloves, he could still get the benefit from the coat. If I lost the cover to the canteen, I lost the benefit of both the cover and the canteen.

In sales, we tie the Attention Step and the Interest Step together so that neither we nor the prospect loses either one. If one of the two is lost, the other is practically worthless. If we do not get the prospect to like us and to focus on us in the Attention Step, we are in trouble. If we get the Attention of the prospect but lose the Interest Step, the prospect does not want to hear about our product.

In Chapter 2 we discussed the salesperson who had, as an Attention Step, a metal beetle that flipped into the air. Next came the Interest Step: The company's thermostats were made of the same two bonded metals. They were just as sensitive to changes in temperature as the beetles, which means the room temperature they controlled would be constant. The two steps are relevant to each other, or tied together.

The candle that lights itself after being blown out was the Attention Step. It is relevant to the Interest Step: Every time the motorist passes the sign again it is visible, unlike other forms of advertising. The story about Joe and Mary Doaks is the Attention Step. It leads right into the benefit that the Doaks received from the company's alarm system. When the prospects hear about the benefits the other people received, they want to hear more about it. That accomplishes the purpose of the Interest Step.

In the Attention Step, where the ball bearing was rolled across the desk of the purchasing agent, the P.A. asked, "What is that for?" Then the salesperson gave the P.A. the Interest Statement, "That ball bearing can save your plant lots of time, and lots of money." That caused the P.A. to want to hear about it, which is the purpose of the Interest Step.

The Attention Step and the Interest Step must be relevant to each other, or tied together. This was fairly easy to do in the above circumstances. They can be prepared ahead of time and rehearsed to make sure they work. There is another situation where we cannot rehearse the two steps prior to the time we make the approach. This is when we are making cold calls, and we do not know what to expect ahead of time. There is, however, a solution to make this situation work well.

Sign of a Smile

Paul, a young salesman in Grand Rapids, Michigan was selling a sales course. He walked into a life insurance agency on a cold call. Having been trained to find an attention getter, he looked around the office and spied a small sign next to the phone that read "Smile." The agency manager asked Paul, "May I help you?" Pointing to the sign,

Chapter 3 Tying Attention and Interest Together

Paul said, "Most people don't realize you can smile on the phone. Was that your idea?" The manager said, "Yes," and explained that he felt it was important to have a smile when talking to a prospect on the phone.

Paul then said, *"The fact that you have* a sign reminding people to smile on the phone *indicates to me that you are the type of person who is constantly on the alert for fresh new ideas to help increase sales. Would that be correct?"* The manager said, "Yes." Paul then added, *"The reason I mention that is because we have a* program coming here to Grand Rapids *that has helped other* sales organizations *much like yours*, with fresh new ideas *to increase sales and earn more profits, and I feel we can do the same for you."* The manager, his interest aroused, said, "Tell me about it," while escorting Paul into his office. (Incidentally, a couple of their agents joined the class.)

That happened 25 years ago. How did I know what Paul said? I trained him in that track. We both knew it verbatim. Paul had practiced. Therefore, he was able to pick something in that office of which the manager was proud. Because he knew the track so well, he was able to smoothly use an indicator to get the manager to state, "Yes, I am interested in fresh new ideas to help increase sales." It was then a simple task to give a General Interest Statement, so the prospect would want to listen.

Remember, the purpose of the Attention Step is to get the prospect to like us and to focus on us. This prospect liked Paul's compliment and focused on him immediately. Not only that, but the compliment on the smile sign was relevant to what Paul was selling. Remember, also, that we have our prospect's Attention only for a fleeting moment, so we must immediately tell them something we can do for them, something they want or need. This is the Interest Step.

People might say Paul was lucky the sign was there. That is not true. There were probably five or ten other items or situations in that office which he could have used just as effectively. Paul was looking for something that the manager was proud of, and the rest was just track. Good salespeople do not depend on luck. They depend on good training in basics, and practice, practice, practice.

How the Indicator Works

Our products have characteristics that are of benefit to prospective clients. The products furnish pride, profit, or value to those clients. For instance, in selling to a sales organization, we look for an Attention-getter that indicates the value, *fresh new ideas for increasing sales*. The Attention-getter may be an award, a diploma on the wall, or any number of items generally found in sales offices.

Let's stroll into a gift shop and pay a compliment on the high quality of the gifts. First, we pay the compliment and then ask if that person is responsible for the high quality of the gifts. If he or she says, "Yes," continue. *"The fact that you have* such a selection of high quality gifts, *indicates to me that you are the type of person who is constantly on the alert for fresh new ideas to help increase sales. Would that be correct?"* The person will say, "Yes." We respond, *"The reason I mention that is because we have* some fresh new ideas in high-quality, hand-crafted gifts *that have helped other* gift stores, *much like yours, to increase sales and earn more profits. I feel we can do the same for you."*

Now, let's go into a store and sell a rubbish removal service. Here the compliment may be on neatness, cleanliness, orderliness, environmental responsibility, or other values to which we can appeal, and that our product will enhance. Again, first ask if this person is responsible for the neat and clean store. If he or she says, "Yes," we say, *"The fact that you have* such a neat, clean store, *indicates to me that you are the type of person who is constantly on the alert for fresh new ideas on how to* appeal to customers to come in here and buy. *Would that be correct?"* "Yes."

Chapter 3 Tying Attention and Interest Together

"The reason I mention that is because we have helped many businesses, *much like yours,* to draw more customers into their stores, and at the same time reduce the cost of their rubbish removal. *I feel we can do the same for you."*

In the examples of using an indicator to tie the first two steps together, the italicized words are the same in each of the three examples. This is a track for tying the Attention Step to the Interest Step in a cold-call situation.

We can be prepared to give an effective approach to just about any type of prospect, regardless of whether we have or lack advance information about the prospect. In order to do this, we must make sure the two steps are tied together, and we must have had enough practice ahead of time to make our presentation flow smoothly.

The next eight chapters are dedicated to determining what our prospects want to achieve, the benefits they want us to talk about, and how to motivate them to gain what it is they want from our products.

CHAPTER 4

THE GENERAL INTEREST STATEMENT

L et's review the five steps of the selling process: Attention, Interest, Desire, Conviction, and Close. We have covered the Attention Step, and tying the Attention Step and Interest Step Together. Now we start learning more about the Interest Step. The purpose of this step is to get the prospect to listen. In other words, mentally we want the prospect to say, "Tell me about your product."

I was talking to a group of real estate agents, and I asked, "What if I could show you how to decrease your income taxes by 25 percent this year?" Then I followed that question with, "I cannot do that, but I'll tell you what I can do. I can show you how to increase your income taxes by 25 percent," knowing that they would realize it would occur as a result of increased income.

There was absolute silence from the group while all ears were tuned in waiting for the magic formula. That was my Interest Statement. I could tell them exactly what I could do for them, because I knew exactly what they were interested in. It did not matter whether they believed me. Regardless of whether or not they believed me, they would listen, just in case I knew what I was talking about. That is the purpose of the Interest Step, to get prospects to listen to us. Ordinarily we cannot use an Interest Statement as specific as that. We must give a General Interest Statement.

The reason we must start with a General Interest Statement is because we do not have the information on what prospects might want from our product, or why that would be important to them. Yet we want them to keep tuned in to us until we can determine that information. Here is the problem we are faced with. We have to tell the prospects what we can do for them, and we are not yet sure of what they want or need. Fortunately, there is a solution.

There are three or four major benefits that people want from just about every product. In the General Interest Statement, we simply tell our prospects that we feel we can help them achieve those benefits. They will listen. Before they have the chance to ask, "How?" we ask for permission to ask questions. Through this questioning, we determine, exactly, the wants and needs of the prospect.

For instance, in Chapter 2 when discussing the Attention Step, there was the story about Kerry Haynor using a Question Bearing on a Need. His Attention Step was, "If there were a way for you to reduce the maintenance required on your boilers, and have them last longer, you would certainly want to know about that, wouldn't you?" The prospects say, "Yes," and then they get the following General Interest Statement: "The reason I mention that is because I feel I can show you how to reduce the maintenance required, have them last longer, and at the same time, reduce your costs."

Let's dissect this General Interest Statement: Three of the major problems with boilers is that they require maintenance, they do not last as long as companies want them to last, and they cost money to maintain. When we tell people with the responsibility of maintaining boilers that we feel we can solve these problems, they listen to us. We do not know for sure that we can give the benefits, so we say we feel we can solve these problems. To come right out and say we can solve the problems is a little brash, and we may get resistance from the prospect, which we do not want.

After we make the General Interest Statement, and before the prospect has a chance to ask, "How?" we say, "In order to determine how much benefit you can receive, and to conserve your time, may I ask you some questions?" They will say, "Yes," because we have told them something we felt we could do for them.

We also told them that we would determine how much benefit they could receive, and that we would conserve their time.

The definition of a prospect is: "someone who has a need, the ability to pay for it, and is willing to listen." The purpose of the General Interest Statement is to get them to listen until we can determine if they have a need and the ability to pay for it.

Earlier in this chapter, it was stated that there are three or four major benefits that people want from just about every product. Usually they will include *quality, reasonable price*, and *suited to their needs*.

Examples of General Interest Statements

- I have helped many other people get *quality* tires that *fit their style* of driving, *at a reasonable price*, and I feel I can do the same for you.

- I have helped many other home buyers like you to find a *quality* home that *fits their needs, at a reasonable price*, and I feel I can do the same for you.

- I have helped many other first-time computer buyers come up with a *quality* system that *fits their needs, at a reasonable price*, and I feel I can do the same for you.

- I have helped many other small businesses like yours obtain *quality* office furniture that *fits their needs, at a reasonable price*, and I feel I can do the same for you. In order to determine how much benefit you can receive, and to conserve your time, may I ask you some questions?

- I have helped many other young couples develop *quality* life insurance programs that *fit their needs, at a reasonable cost*, and I feel that I can do the same for you. In order to determine how much benefit you can receive, and to conserve your time, may I ask you some questions?

John Bryan with Long Real Estate Company was trying to get an appointment with a prospect who had been unsuccessful in finding 10,000 square feet of warehouse on a short-term lease. The prospect started to dismiss John by telling of the number of agents he had already worked with who told him that it was impossible. John said, "Mr._____, I have helped many other businessmen, much like you, find quality properties that fit their needs at a reasonable price, and I feel I can do the same for you." John got the appointment and asked the questions the other agents had not asked. He determined how to solve the prospect's problem rather than just trying to make a sale. As a result, he made the sale.

Some products are different

"I have helped many other home owners much like you, who are moving up to a larger home, to sell their homes quickly, get the maximum amount of money for it, and do so with very little bother to them. In order to determine how much benefit you can receive, and to conserve your time, may I ask you some questions?"

"We have helped many home owners like you, who do not have the time to work on the lawn, have healthy lawns, maintained in the style they want, at a reasonable cost, and I feel I can do the same for you. In order to determine how much benefit you can receive, and to conserve your time, may I ask you some questions?"

Notice in the last example, I started with the pronoun "we." Some salespeople prefer it that way, especially new salespeople, who feel they have not personally helped many others.

Remember in the last chapter, Paul got the Attention of the manager of the life insurance agency, and then used the indicator to relate the Smile sign to a reason to take a sales course. Here is the General Interest Statement that Paul used: "We have a program coming here to Grand Rapids that has helped other sales organizations, much like yours, with fresh new ideas to increase sales, and earn more profits, and I feel we can do the same for you."

Notice that in all of these examples of General Interest Statements, we do not tell the prospects we can give them these benefits. At this time we do not know what we can do for them. The purpose of the General Interest Statement is to get prospects to listen to us. Of course before they hear us tell them specifically what we can do for them, we will ask them some questions.

We tell how we have helped many others, *much like you. . . .* This tells the prospects that they are not alone, but that we have worked with people similar to them or their business. We do not say, others *exactly like you,* because there are no others exactly like them. We want our prospects to be comfortable with the knowledge that they are working with the right salesperson, someone who has worked with people, *much like them,* before.

Some people say that this is the shotgun approach to selling. If I tell my prospects buying tires that I can get them quality tires suitable to their style of driving, at a reasonable cost, and do not get information from them to find out their particular needs, it is a shotgun approach. With a shotgun approach, I will not sell many tires nor will I serve my clients well. The purpose of this General Interest Statement is not to sell our product to the prospects, but to get them interested enough to listen. When they are ready to listen, we ask permission to ask them some questions.

The Bridge to Information

Let's look at "In order to determine how much benefit you can receive, and to conserve your time, may I ask you some questions." Notice we do not say *if* they can receive benefit, but *how much* benefit they can receive. We also say to *conserve* your time, rather than *save* it. It is easier to conserve than to save. If you feel more at ease with your own wording, do so as long as it doesn't change the meaning.

This question is called the Bridge to Information because we bridge over from the General Interest Statement to the Information gathering phase. For almost thirty years, I have asked that question of prospects. In all those years, not one of them has said "No."

Ask for permission to ask questions and prospects will grant that permission if you have given them a good reason to in your General Interest Statement. If you look at your prospects immediately after asking the Bridge to Information, you will find they will be looking directly at you, waiting for you to continue. That is a nice feeling when giving a sales presentation.

The phone call for an appointment is similar to the Attention and Interest Steps in nose-to-nose selling (as discussed in the first three chapters). On the phone it is even more important to get prospects' minds off of what they were on before we called. We use an Attention Step to get them to focus on what we are saying, and a General Interest Statement telling them what we feel we can do for them. Then, rather than asking for permission to gather information, we ask for the appointment.

Review of the General Interest Statement

When the executive went into his office, he was met by the receptionist. She told him that he had two phone calls asking for appointments. She said, "One was from the snake man who wants to sell you some poisonous snakes. The other was a salesman who wants to show you some of his company's products." The executive thought for a moment, then asked, "Did the snake man leave a number where I can reach him?"

The point of this story is: Prospects would rather see a snake man than a salesman who wants to show his products. Prospects do not care about our company or our products. They care about their companies and their products. To get an appointment we must talk in terms of the problems they have that we can solve.

I was talking one day to a man in the kitchen cabinet business. Actually I was listening to him complain about it. He said,

"I go to their homes, find out what they want, measure their kitchens, and give them an estimate. I do all that, and then they want the highest quality at the lowest price." He is absolutely right. That is what they want, not what they buy all the time, but *what they want*. Remember that! Because if we want prospects to listen to our presentation, in the General Interest Statement we must talk about *what they want*, *quality*, *reasonable price*, and *suited to their needs*.

Here Is Our Track So Far:

- Attention Step

- Indicator (Optional)

- General Interest Statement

- Bridge to Information

In Using the Phone to Get an Appointment:

- Attention Step

- Indicator (Optional)

- General Interest Statement

- Ask for the Appointment

Next: Information Gathering (Info)

CHAPTER 5

INFORMATION GATHERING (Info)

I was invited to a hotel one day to hear a sales trainer talk to about 200 of his salespeople. His name was Bud. Here is his story.

Seek First to Understand

Bud moved into the suburbs after his promotion. With the home came a large lawn, so he had to buy a mower. He went into a hardware store and the clerk came up to him and asked, "May I help you?" Fortunately for the clerk, Bud said, "Yes, I'm looking for a mower." The clerk asked what kind he was looking for, and Bud said he was not sure. Unfortunately, the clerk said, "There are a bunch of them over there. Take a look at them and call me if you need some help." Bud looked at them and left the store.

Bud saw another store with mowers so he stopped there. The clerk approached him and asked if he could help him. Again, Bud said, "Yes, I'm looking for a mower." The clerk asked what kind he was looking for, and Bud said he was not sure. Fortunately, the clerk then asked Bud how large his lawn was. Bud said, "Almost two acres." The clerk said, "Then you probably should have a mower that cuts a wide swath, so it doesn't take you all day to mow the lawn." The clerk then asked if the lawn was flat or hilly. Bud told him it was basically flat, but sloped down to the road along the front. The sales clerk said, "You should have a mower with a powerful engine so you can make it up that slope. That way, you don't have to buy a hand mower." He then asked who would be using the mower. Bud said, "I will now, but I have two children who are getting to the age where they will want to mow." The clerk said, "You will want a mower with ample safety features so your children are protected."

The sales clerk took Bud over to a mower and told him it cut a wide swath so he would not have to spend all day mowing; it was powerful enough to make it up the slope so he would not have to buy a hand mower; and that it had several safety features so his children would be safe while mowing.

Bud told his salespeople that he bought the mower. He then told the moral to his tale: *People Do Not Buy Our Product Because They Understand It. They Buy Our Product Because We Understand Them.* In twenty-five years of studying selling and training in selling, I never heard it stated so well.

Something else is interesting about Bud's story. The sales clerk never talked about his product until he found the information he needed, the prospect's problem. This is important because how in the world can we start solving someone's problem unless we first find out what that problem is?

Selling Is Not Telling

So many times when prospects start telling why they would be interested in our products, we get excited and have the tendency to start telling them that we can do what they want done. Resist! Keep listening until they finish telling. At the 1994 Sales & Marketing Executives International Convention in Norfolk, Virginia, Dr. Steven Covey, author of *The Seven Habits of Highly Effective People,* stated, "Seek first to understand, not to be understood."

While I was an Area Manager for The Dale Carnegie Course, a new salesperson was sent to help me sell in my territory. He had taken the class and was very excited about the enthusiasm he had gained from the experience. Because of that, management felt he would do well.

He did not sell well. He was so excited about having increased his enthusiasm that he had to tell every prospect and every company about it. He liked the course because it helped him build his enthusiasm, but people do not buy products because of what the salesperson likes.

He was trying to get others to understand what he was saying about the course rather than trying to understand what they wanted to receive. As a result, not only did he have poor sales performance but he ruined many prospects for me. Many times I would call on a company only to find that this excited salesman had already tried to sell them on an enthusiasm course that they did not want.

He would talk to twelve prospects a day and sell one of them. I would call on half that number and sign up three or four. He did not last because he did not try to find out what his prospects were interested in, but only told what he was interested in. He was telling rather than selling.

In seeking to understand, we simply ask questions of prospects instead of telling them what we can do for them with our products. Many times the answers are enlightening and completely different from what is expected.

I was one of the speakers at a state convention of business managers which was being held at a large hotel in a major city. In preparation for one of the sales meetings, the management of the hotel where the all day event was being held was asked what kind of service conventioneers expected at their coffee breaks. The answer was that they wanted silver service and nice china on white draped tables.

The same question was asked on a questionnaire given to the business managers who attended the convention. The answer they gave was that they wanted their coffee in Styrofoam cups close to telephones and rest rooms. At the first break they were treated to silver service and nice china on white draped tables.

When I met Thane Belen, he was working as a sales clerk in a department store. I was interested in hiring him as an insurance agent, but what he really wanted was to sell real estate. While questioning him I had discovered that he loved selling, but required supervision to make sure he did what he was supposed to do. He realized this, so he was looking for a company that would give him close supervision and require him to put what he learned into practice.

I knew of a company that combined lots of sales training and close supervision. The sales manager, Dave, was almost like a mother hen to the agents, supervising them closely to make sure they did what they were supposed to do. Thane was interested in talking to him, so I set up a breakfast meeting between him and Dave.

At the meeting after the preliminary pleasantries were completed, Dave started telling this prospective agent what he thought was important about his company. He was telling what a nice easygoing place it was, and how the agents were like a big family, when I stopped him and said, "Please let me ask a question." With his approval I asked Thane, "What is it that you are looking for in a real estate company?"

He answered, "I want a company that has continuous training and close supervision to make me do what I am capable of doing." I asked him why that was important to him, and he replied that he was used to working under a time clock and would need someone to stay on his back and push him to learn and work until he became successful.

I then asked Dave, "Can you do that for him?" Dave said that he could. I then told Thane, "He says that he can do that for you. Do you want to work with him?" Thane said, "Yes." Then I told Dave, "He says he would like to work with you. Why don't you take him to the office and sign him up after we finish breakfast?"

Dave said, "OK." After we finished breakfast Dave took Thane to the office and started the contracting paperwork.

Dave was used to people who wanted to sell real estate because it was easy. He was assuming that was important to Thane and was completely wrong. He was about to blow the interview by assuming instead of asking questions.

People are different; so in order to determine what others want in a product we have to ask questions. The problem is that so many times we know what we like, and we assume that others feel the same way. And so many times when we assume, we are wrong. Do not assume. Ask!

There are those in the life insurance industry that base their entire presentation on the premise that there is no reason to buy life insurance other than purely as protection. That is not why I bought it, nor why I have it now. Some say that the purpose of an automobile is only to provide transportation. They never knew my son Scott, who said, "I would rather have a car that I like, even if it doesn't run, than one that runs, that I don't like."

If you believe the only purpose of a tie clip is to keep your tie out of your soup, perhaps you should use a paper clip. Try that the next time you go on a dinner date. It would cause less trouble than if you try to sell by telling prospects what they do not want to hear. Really, people have their own reasons to buy, and they are happy to tell us what those reasons are, if we ask them properly.

Ask

I talked to a woman once who wanted her sixteen-year-old son to take the Dale Carnegie Course so he would be more effective on the school debate team. I assured her that he would receive the benefit she wanted for him, if he made his own decision to join the course. She agreed to pay for it.

I did not sell him on doing better on the debate team, because he only could be motivated to join for his own reasons. I discovered in the Information Gathering that he wanted to be more at ease when talking to girls. I told him that after completing the class, he would be more at ease when talking to girls, and he agreed to join. The sale was made, and they both received the benefits they wanted, only because I found out what each of them wanted.

When I told this story in a class, somebody asked, "Do you mean that this woman paid money for her son to take a class to be more at ease when talking to girls?" I told the person who asked, "No, she paid money for him to do better on the debate team. She received the benefit she wanted."

Not only do people buy for their own reasons, but different people will buy the same product for different reasons, and each will receive the benefits they want.

I cannot tell people why they should buy my product without first asking them questions. Some people say, "It is your product. Tell me what it will do for me." They are right. It is my product, but I am smart enough to know that people buy my product for their reasons, not mine.

Even if we know a person is not a prospect, we should ask questions. Bob Scott, with Robert W. Baird & Co. Inc., sent me a note from Phoenix, Arizona, where he talked with a young single woman who had no need for his life insurance products. He said he did an Information Gathering anyway and found that she was trustee of her mother's estate, valued at $500,000. She was unhappy with the management of the trust assets, and Bob ended up with a nice sale and a nice commission.

There are times that salespeople start a presentation with the idea of selling one product and end up selling another. While questioning the prospect, they suddenly realize that they should make the change based on the information they get.

In 1984 Dennis Grim started "Business to Business Communications" in Elgin, Illinois, selling to the transportation industry. He said that his present program, *Transportation Digest,* an audio news magazine, was developed by listening during his first presentation to a major railroad.

Grim said that while being told why the railroad would not use his service, his thoughts were, "Here is a sale if I allow it; not selling what I came in to sell, but selling what they want to buy." He listened his way into a program that over the years has been distributed to an audience of more than 12,000 listeners.

There are salespeople who make their calls without any idea what product they will be selling until after they have completed the information gathering. There are salespeople who do not even have a product to sell when they make a sales call.

Mike Devaney, who sold for Ciba-Geigey, made calls on aircraft manufacturers without a product to sell. He talked to their engineers to discover what problems they had in manufacturing. Then he would return to his plant and have his chemists develop a product to solve their problems.

The Right Way to Get the Right Information

How do we gather information? In the last chapter, we learned to ask for it, along with giving a couple of carrots to the prospect in return for permission to ask: "In order to determine how much benefit you can receive, and to conserve your time, may I ask you some questions?"

Not to ask permission may seem rude to prospects or perhaps confuse them. Here they were expecting a presentation of why they should buy our product, and we start asking questions. We want to be on the same track as the prospect, advancing smoothly toward the sale. Ask their permission to ask questions and they will say, "Yes."

We get information on which to base a presentation from many sources, but here we will discuss only one source, the prospect. We gather information from our prospect, or we have the prospect confirm information we received from another source. This process of information gathering is called the *"Info."* In the Info, we ask Fact-Finding and Feeling-Finding questions.

In Fact-Finding, we generally get the answers to background questions we need to determine the prospect's situation. In Feeling-Finding, we determine the logical and emotional answers from prospects that will motivate them to buy. The logical answers and the emotional answers are so closely related that many times we ask a question to get logic and we get an emotion for the answer, or when we are looking for an emotion we get a logical answer.

It is important for us to know the difference between logical and emotional answers because they serve different purposes. For instance, if I am looking for an emotional reason for the prospect to buy, the prospect may answer in logic, which may be nice to know, but I still want the emotional response. I must ask again. It is the response that is important rather than the question.

I may never ask a Feeling-Finding question, but prospects may give me all the benefits and emotional reasons to want the product right now. If I ask the standard questions when I already have the information, the prospect will know I have not been listening. And if I was not listening, I miss the way to get the prospect to buy.

Some people say to sell the sizzle, not the steak. Why not sell both? A steak without sizzle may be boring, but a sizzle without steak is nothing. I believe what they mean is to sell the steak (Logic) and the sizzle (Emotion). People 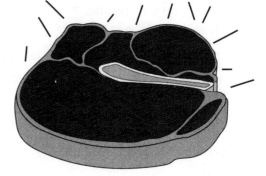 buy for logical and emotional reasons to varying degrees, and we had better talk about both if we want to talk in terms of the buyers' interests.

Fact-Finding Questions

Which questions come first? The Fact-Finding. In the Fact Finding we ask the nonthreatening background questions first. We do not want to startle the prospects by first asking them how much money they owe on credit cards, or even how much money they earn. When the prospects are families or individuals, we can start by asking about them, their children, their homes, or their work.

When working with a business, we can ask nonthreatening background questions about the business, such as how long it has been in business, what it manufactures, etc. Also, we can ask personal questions of the buyer. This morning I met with a business manager, and we talked about our children for a couple of minutes. Then we talked about how the company got started and how it progressed over the years. Much of it was small talk, but most of it was information necessary to get a better idea of what I might be able to do for the business. It was all nonthreatening.

Later on, after the light questioning, we can bridge over into more "threatening" background questions. How much the prospect owes, his or her income, problems and such. With a business we can inquire about financial matters and those of a more confidential nature. Here we gather the facts that we need to make a sale. It is background information we need in order to do a reasonable job in making sure we know what the prospect is interested in.

If we are talking about tires for a car, some of the facts we need to know are the size of the tires, whether they are specialty tires for mud or snow or mostly highway driving, and how long the prospects expect to keep the tires or the car.

Background questions are generally asked at the beginning of the questioning process. They are similar to small talk. As when meeting a new friend, we start with small talk until we become more comfortable with each other. In the Info, background questions help us to continue building a comfortable relationship.

Feeling-Finding Questions

At this stage, prospects will tell us which product to talk about and how to present it to them. Here is where the prospects tell us what their primary interest is in our product, the specific benefits of our product that they want to hear about, and how to motivate them to buy it.

Primary Interest: What particular aspect about our product is of primary interest to the prospect.

Specific Benefits: What benefits of our product the prospect is specifically interested in.

Dominant Buying Motive: The emotion that will move the prospect to buy our product.

Our entire presentation, up to this point, is to get this information: their primary interest in our product, the specific benefits they want to achieve, and their dominant motivation to take action. Everything we say and do from this point on is based on that information.

The Standard Feeling-Finding Questions

While in Los Angeles attending the wedding of friends, I stayed at the Hyatt at the Los Angeles Airport. The last day prior to check-out time I received a thank-you card and an evaluation form. The form asked what I enjoyed most about my stay at the Hyatt, what I may have disliked about my stay there, and what I would suggest they change to make my next stay there more enjoyable.

You may recognize these three standard Feeling-Finding questions from questionnaires you have received after a stay at a hotel or hospital. They are meant to evaluate the service. They are the same questions colleges and universities use to evaluate their instruction. They are problem-finding questions. They are the same questions we should ask in Customer-Driven Sales.

- What do you like most about . . . ?

- What do you dislike most about . . . ?

- If I could change something about . . . , what would you want to be different?

For example: *What do you like most about your present supplier?* Here prospects tell us what we are up against if we try to replace their present supplier. They are saying, "You had better be able to do this as well as they do."

What do you dislike most about your present supplier? Here they tell us what our competition is doing wrong. They are saying, "Here is the problem I have with my present supplier. Solve this problem and we may do business."

If we were to be your supplier, what would you want us to do differently than is presently being done? Here they tell us what they are primarily interested in if they change suppliers. It is their evaluation of how to solve the problem from the previous question. There they said, "Solve this problem and you are on the way to getting my business." Here they tell you how to get their business.

Ask Why

Now we know the bare facts about the prospect's problem and how to solve it. Look what happens to these three questions when we add the question "Why?" after each one.

Bob sells carpet. He travels all over the state, does his own installing, and has a choice of 500 different carpets. He says that those three facts are important to his clients, so that is what he tells all of them.

Once I asked Bob to try an experiment on one client, to use the three standard Feeling-Finding questions—Like, Dislike, and Change—and ask the question "Why?" after each of them. This is what he reported back.

He asked a woman what she liked most about her present carpet. She said she liked the fact that when it was new, the nap stood up straight and looked nice. When asked why that was important to her, she said it was important so her home looked nice when she had parties.

Bob asked her what she disliked most about the present carpet. She replied that after it was cleaned the nap went flat and did not look as nice as when it was new. He asked why that was a problem for her. She said that each time it was cleaned, it looked worse than it had before; so she had to choose between buying new carpeting or having ugly carpeting. Bob asked again why that was a problem. She said, "My thing is giving parties, and I want people to compliment my home, rather than notice my old carpet."

Bob then asked her if she could have something different in her next carpeting, what would it be? She instantly replied that she wanted carpet where the nap would continue to stand up straight after it was cleaned. He asked her why that was important to her, and again she told him how she loved to hear nice things about her home and her furnishings. "I want to be proud of my home, not ashamed."

I asked Bob if he had told her he installed his own carpet, traveled all over the state, and had a selection of 500 different carpets. He said, "No."

That woman did not want 500 different carpets, she did not care who traveled all over the state, or even who installed it. She just wanted some carpeting where the nap continued standing up straight after it had been cleaned.

I do not know what Bob told her, but what he should have promised would be something like this: "You buy from me and I will give you carpet where the nap will stand up when it is new, and will continue to stand up straight after it has been cleaned." (*That was her Primary Interest.*) "You won't have to make the decision to pay for new carpet or have ugly carpeting. You will have nice looking carpet, and at your parties, people will say nice things about your home." (*Those were the Specific Benefits she wanted.*) "You will be proud, rather than ashamed." (*That was her Dominant Buying Motive.*)

Notice how the answers went from Primary Interest, the logic of having nap that stood up, to the logic (Specific Benefits) she wanted of having nice-looking carpet and people saying nice things about her home, to Dominant Buying Motive, the emotion of wanting to be proud, not ashamed. The promise that Bob should have made to the prospect fit her specific needs. We know that because she gave him the information. It is called a Specific Promise. We will discuss it later in Chapter 9.

Jack was a real estate agent in Kalamazoo, Michigan. He was enrolled in a sales class that I taught. My family and I were leaving Kalamazoo and Jack made a presentation to list our house for sale. Because I was teaching these standard Feeling-Finding questions, he knew he had to ask them of me if he wanted to make the sale. Here is how it went.

Jack asked if I had ever listed a home through a real estate agent before. I told him, "Yes." He asked what I liked most about the person who listed my home. I told him that the agent was an acquaintance, and that my wife and I liked him as a person. He asked why that was important to me, and I told him that we enjoyed doing business with people we liked, and especially with people we knew.

Jack then asked what I disliked most about the agent who had listed our home. I told Jack that after it was listed, we never saw or heard from him again. Jack asked me why that was a problem for me. I told him basically, "People would go through our home, look at it, and then leave. We never knew if they liked it, if there was something wrong with it, or if there was something else we should be doing. We had a tough time contacting the agent to find out anything."

Then Jack asked, "If there were something you would want me to change or do differently in helping you sell your home, what would that be?" I told him that we would want to be notified of what took place every time someone looked at the house, either good or bad comments. Jack asked why that was important to me. I remember the answer well. "In the evening after people looked at the house, my wife would ask if I found out what they thought of the house, or if they made an offer." Of course I would have to say, 'No.' And she would say to me, 'You hired him.'"

We had not intended to list the house that evening, but when Jack told me that he would find out what he could and get back to us every time anyone went through the house (my Primary Interest), we were interested. Then he said he would keep me supplied with enough information that I would know if people who went through the home liked it, and I would know if there was anything else we should be doing (the Specific Benefits I wanted). Then he said the best part, that I wouldn't have to hear, "You hired him," any more (my Dominant Buying Motive).

I signed the listing agreement. Not only was I happy to do so, but my wife was happy, too. Jack worked hard at selling the house and kept his promise about contacting us.

Jack did not have to tell me that they had twenty agents, that they were a member of the multiple listing service, that they would advertise our home, or hold open houses. We knew that. He found out what our problem was, and told us how he would solve it. And I was the one who told him how to do it when I answered his standard Feeling-Finding questions.

Not only was Jack interested in learning what I felt was necessary to help sell the home, but he also found out what my personal problem was. I did not want to have to listen to the phrase, "You hired him." My wife did not want to have to wonder what people thought of the house. He responded to our feelings and problems by asking the question, "Why?"

Not all of the stories I have heard about asking Feeling-Finding questions are success stories. Doug Alchin is the manager of one of the larger real estate companies in my town. He told me this story.

Two agents with another company were about to make a change. Doug was impressed with their abilities, and tried to recruit them to sell for him. Doug said he knew that the company the two were leaving was family run, so when he made his presentation to them, he stressed the fact that though his company was quite large, it still had family ties.

A few weeks after the two agents made the decision to join a different company, Doug saw one of them. He asked the agent why they had decided to go there instead of with him. The agent said, "We liked your company but the reason we are leaving our previous company is that we are sick of family companies."

Doug said that he feels that if he had known how to ask the standard Feeling-Finding questions when he interviewed the two, he would have been able to get them licensed with his company. He had made the mistake of telling them about his company rather than finding out what they wanted.

Review

Start with nonthreatening Fact-Finding questions, move to the more "threatening" Fact-Finding questions, and then bridge over to the following Feeling-Finding questions:

- What do you like most about your present or last product?

- Why is that important to you?

- What do you dislike most about your present or last product?

- Why is that a problem for you?

- If I could change something for you in your next product, what would you want me to do differently?

- Why would that be important to you?

By the time we finish with these questions, we will know the prospect's *Primary Interest* (the steak) and the benefits the prospect wants to achieve. Then after asking "Why?" a couple of times, we will know what *Specific Benefits* the prospect is looking for. Then we continue the questioning until we arrive at the prospect's *Dominant Buying Motive* (the sizzle).

While in St. Louis, Missouri, I watched a demonstration by a policeman and dog that worked as a team to locate drugs in luggage. The dog got very excited when she detected the smell of drugs in the demonstration. As soon as the dog started digging excitedly where the smell was coming from, the policeman took a tennis ball from his pocket and threw it. The dog took after it immediately.

Both the policeman and the dog wanted the same thing, to locate drugs in shipment, but they wanted to locate them for different reasons. The police wanted to catch smugglers, but the dog really did not care about smugglers, she wanted the chance to play with the tennis ball.

The point to remember is that if we want people to do something, we cannot expect them to want to do so for our reasons. Find out what it is that they want, then we can get them to do what we want for their reasons.

Here is our track so far:

- Attention Step

- Indicator (Optional)

- General Interest Statement

- Bridge to Info

- Fact-Finding Questions

- Standard Feeling-Finding Questions

The purpose of all this is to determine the prospect's Primary Interest, Specific Benefits, and Dominant Buying Motive.

CHAPTER 6

THE PRIMARY INTEREST

People buy our product, not for the product itself, but for the benefits they receive from it. People take medicine for relief, not because they want the medicine. I bought a hole puncher, not because I want a hole puncher, but because I want holes in the edge of my paper. I am not interested in having a computer, I want to be able to write this book. I wanted the computer for other purposes, but I was primarily interested in making sure I could use it for writing.

People are different. They like different aspects of our products, so in order to satisfy them, we have to know "what" those aspects are that they like about our product. They may like many qualities of the product, but usually there is something of primary interest to them. If we do not determine what it is that they want most, someone else will do so and will sell them.

The Way to Find Out Is to Ask

I have heard the expression "buyers are liars" so many times from real estate salespeople. So much of the time, it is simply that the salesperson does not find what the prospect is primarily interested in, the Primary Interest.

A realtor in one of my sales classes was looking for a home for a friend. The friend said she wanted two acres of land, but ended up buying a home with only three-quarters of an acre from someone else. The realtor was angry. I asked her why her friend bought three-quarters of an acre when she said she wanted two acres.

The realtor said, "She wanted room for a horse, and found three-quarters of an acre that already had a barn and a run for a horse. I didn't know why she wanted two acres."

It is our job to ask questions to find out what the prospect wants from our product. In this case the salesperson did not know the prospect's Primary Interest in the land. The person who did find the Primary Interest made the sale of the property.

The woman who bought the home was interested in other aspects of the property. Perhaps in price, location, style, number of rooms, layout, or any number of other factors that are important to home buyers. In this case she was primarily interested in a shelter and run for her horse.

There is a cute saying in real estate sales that the three most important qualities that people look for in buying a home are location, location, and location. The truth is that some home buyers have never heard of that saying. It is better to ask first. Another cute saying was coined by Dave Zydbel who said, "I found there is a difference between being a realtor and being a salesperson."

I bought a car that had some sort of a vibration. I took it back to the dealer, and the dealer said it was the tires. I took it to the tire dealer, and they said it was the car. I decided that buying new tires would cost me less than a new car, so I went tire shopping.

I read that radial tires were very smooth riding and did not vibrate like the type of tires I had. I decided to buy some. I walked into a store that sold radial tires and told the salesperson that I wanted a set for my car. He said, "They are rough riding, but they are great tires." I turned around and walked out, because I wanted smooth-riding tires,

not rough-riding tires. My Primary Interest was smooth-riding tires.

Before we say anything about our product and what it will do for prospects, we must find out what it is they want done.

Products have many benefits or features important to prospective buyers. Usually, there is one feature or benefit that is of primary interest. In getting a set of tires, I wanted safe tires, I wanted something that would be good for both winter and summer driving, I wanted tires that would look nice, but primarily, I was interested in eliminating that annoying vibration.

That would have been so easy for the salesperson to determine, if he had just asked what I liked most about my previous tires, what I disliked about them, and what I would want to be different in my next set of tires. Then he could have sold me the radials that I wanted, and we both would have been happy.

Same Product, Different Problems

When I sold banquet catering, people would call and ask for a price. They would specify a menu and ask me what we would charge for that type of banquet. I would give them a price. They would say, "Thank you." Then they would hang up and I would never hear from them again.

That is when I took a sales class and learned how to sell. When someone called for a price, I would ask what the occasion was. I would find a way to get their Attention and then give a General Interest Statement: "We have helped many other people, much like you, to put on banquets with quality food and service, at a reasonable price, and helped them make their banquets successful. There is no charge for our assistance in planning. In order to determine how much benefit you can receive, when could we meet?"

If they met with me, I would find out what they wanted and help them accomplish it. If they did not wish to meet with me, I would simply ask for permission to ask questions on the phone. They generally would say, "Yes." Then I would do the Info on the phone. I could get just about all the banquets I wanted that way, because I was finding out their problems and solving them.

Interestingly enough, I learned something I should have known already. Obviously, banquets for banks, for religious organizations, or for wedding receptions would have completely different problems. What I did not realize was that banquets for similar purposes would have completely different problems. Once I learned this, I could determine what those problems were. The prospects would even tell me how I could help them solve those problems when I asked the right questions. *Those callers didn't want a price; they wanted a successful banquet.* It sounds so simple now, but I had to learn that.

The questions to determine a prospect's Primary Interest are basically the same regardless of the product. They are problem-finding questions. Here are a few of the problems that I solved for people who wanted banquets.

- It took too long to serve the dinner; some were finished while others were just starting. They blamed me. Primary Interest: Serve the dinner quickly.

- The food was cold. People complained to me, and I was embarrassed. Primary Interest: Serve hot food.

- They ran out of silverware, and some of the guests had to eat with spoons. My daughter was not proud of the reception. Primary Interest: Have enough silverware to go around.

- They did not serve when they were supposed to, and I had to spend much of my time in the kitchen, when I should have been with the guests. I did not enjoy myself. Primary Interest: Serve when you are supposed to.

- They didn't clean up when they finished, so we had to return there to clean up the next day. Primary Interest: Clean up when you are finished.

Notice that none of these problems have anything to do with the menu or the price. We have to ask: What did you like most about the last banquet you had or attended? What did you dislike most about the last banquet you had or attended? If we could do something different to help you have a successful banquet, what would that be?

When we ask those Standard Feeling-Finding questions, we will find what problems our prospects have had in the past. Also we will discover how to solve those problems in order to do a better job serving them.

Obviously all of the problems listed in the above examples were important not to experience in a banquet. Most people want dinner served quickly and on time, served hot, with ample silverware, and they want their facility left clean. Their Primary Interest is that they do not want to relive the problems they experienced in the past

Price is of prime importance, but not what they are buying. *Really, if your daughter were getting married, which would be more important to you, saving a dollar a plate, or having a reception you and your daughter would be proud of?* (I ask this question of you, the reader, not the person booking the banquet.) What would be your Primary Interest?

One Big Surprise

Always determine the Primary Interest before telling someone what they will like about your product. If you do not, most of the time you will be wasting your time and the time of your client. If you determine the Primary Interest first, much of the time you will be surprised that it is not what you thought it would be.

While in the banquet catering business, occasionally we catered at a civic center. They had their own kitchens, but most of their banquets were catered by one of the four major banquet catering companies in town. The center had rooms that would seat from ten to over 4,000 people for a meal. The management of the center did not care who catered the meals, so hiring a caterer was the responsibility of the organization or group who was having the function.

Occasionally we would cater a number of functions consecutively for one group. Once we served meals for an association with over 2,000 people in attendance. We served them 2,500 lunches and dinners on Friday, a slightly larger number for breakfast, lunch, and dinner on Saturday, and breakfast and lunch on Sunday. It was profitable business, and easy to accomplish because of the facilities present at the center.

One day the manager of the civic center called and asked to meet with me. When I got to his office, he proceeded to tell me that he would offer us a contract that essentially stated, "Any organization that wanted to use the rooms of the civic center for banquet purposes, would be required to use the catering company that [I] managed."

This meant that we had no competition to worry about. This meant that we could charge a fair price but not have to worry about getting into a bidding war. This meant that we could do jobs with less effort because we could then lock up some of our equipment there. This meant that we could more than double our business in one fell swoop.

I was dumbfounded and had no idea of the reasoning behind the decision. I wondered what his Primary Interest was, so I did what any red-blooded American salesperson should have done. I asked, "Why?"

The manager took me into one of their kitchens and showed me the mess that another catering company had left after feeding a group. He told me that they checked after every banquet and found that my company did a better job of cleanup than any other caterer that used the facilities. That was his Primary Interest.

He did not want a deal; he was not that concerned about the food that was served, nor the efficiency of our operation; he did not even seem to be concerned about how happy the end-users were with our food and service. He simply wanted a caterer who would leave the facilities clean. I am sure he wanted us to give their groups good food and service at a fair price, but what he was primarily interested in was that his facilities be left clean.

I was lucky. If I had been smart I would have made a presentation to him without waiting for him to contact me, and in the process I would have discovered the problem he was having. Almost everyone has a problem of some sort that we can solve, and it is our job as salespeople to determine what problems we can solve with our products. Usually this is quite easy to do simply by asking the Standard Feeling-Finding questions.

There are times we do not have to ask any questions in order to determine a prospect's Primary Interest. Occasionally prospects will tell what it is at the beginning. They might tell what the biggest problem is that they have in their business. When they do that, it does not make sense to ask the question. The answer we are looking for is important (The Primary Interest), not the question.

There are times when we cannot get the Primary Interest simply by using the Standard Feeling-Finding questions. Perhaps because the prospect is not familiar with our product or has no past experience on which to base answers. Perhaps it is a new product. Perhaps we find the prospect has had no real problem in the past. Sometimes we will want to delve deeper simply because it is an important account. There is a way to find the Primary Interest, no matter what the circumstances. We can use a menu, which will be discussed in Chapter 10.

CHAPTER 7

SPECIFIC BENEFITS

L iving in a General Motors town, I have always been under quite a bit of pressure to buy an automobile produced locally. A few years ago I was about to buy a sporty car built by another of the American auto manufacturers. An acquaintance of mine named Bob, who was selling for a local GM dealership, asked to have a chance to sell me before I made the final commitment.

Bob had been through a sales class that taught him not only to give facts but to follow each fact with a benefit. I remember him telling me about his car that had a larger trunk so I could carry  more luggage, a larger interior so I could carry more passengers, a car that was heavier so the ride would be more comfortable, a larger gas tank so I would not have to stop as often for gas, and a host of other wonderful benefits.

At the end he even mentioned that the car that I wanted to buy probably would not sell many units, and therefore I would be driving a car that was different from what anybody else would be driving.

That last fact and benefit made up my mind for me. I went ahead with my purchase of that sporty little car. That was exactly what I wanted, a car that was different from what everybody else in town was driving.

Bob gave me all the facts and benefits that were important to him. They meant absolutely nothing to me. Not only was I not interested in what he was talking about, but I was bored. I was also angry because he was trying to sell me a car that he wanted to sell me, with no concern for what I wanted.

Benefits Must be Specific to the Buyer

Rule 3 of *The 5 Great Rules of Selling* by Percy Whiting states: "Give your prospect enough facts, and no more, about your product and how it will benefit him, to convince him that he is justified in buying."

Notice that it states, "how it will benefit *him*." This means only those facts and benefits that are important to the prospect, not to the salesperson, the guy next door, the builder, the owner, or anyone else; only to the prospect. And it states, "and no more." Those are Specific Benefits, benefits that are specific to the prospect or the buyer.

I recently read in a sales magazine that one of the major auto companies had decided to push benefits rather than just giving facts about their automobiles. The article listed a bunch of example benefits that their salespeople could use. As I remember, none of those benefits applied to me. The last time I listened to a salesperson at their local dealership tell me reasons I should buy their car, none of those reasons were important to me either.

There is no reason to fall into the trap of boring or angering prospects by talking to them about benefits in which they are not interested. If we do, we are causing objections, because they will say, "That is not important to me," or worse yet, they won't tell us, but will hold it inside, where it will become a reason not to buy.

It is so easy to find out what is important to prospects simply by asking. They will tell us specifically what they are interested in, and what they are not interested in. Then we can tell them specifically what benefits they can expect to receive from our products and not be the cause of objections.

Once we discover any aspect of our product that is of interest to prospects, all we have to do to determine the benefits they want is to ask the following question: "Why is that important to you?" They will tell us.

Back in Chapter 5, Information Gathering, it was stated that we solicit both logical and emotional responses to Feeling-Finding questions, and that it is important to know the difference. Here is why: The logical answers are Specific Benefits that are to be derived from the product, and they are product related. The emotional answers are not product related. They are not derived from the product, but from the person. An emotional response is the Dominant Buying Motive. More on that in the next chapter.

For now let's discuss Specific Benefits, the logical reasons that cause people to want to buy.

Real Live Examples

I was talking to a salesperson about a sales class. Her Primary Interest was to do a better job of closing.

- I asked her why she would want to do a better job closing. Answer—Specific Benefit: So she could get more people to make the decision to buy right now.

- I asked how that would benefit her. Answer—Specific Benefit: So she could make more sales and more money.

- I asked why making more money would be important to her. Answer—Specific Benefit: She said that besides selling real estate, she was working another full-time job. That gave her the money to live on until she earned enough in real estate to make it with one job.

- I asked why it was so important to be able to quit the old job. Answer—Specific Benefit: She said that she was tired of working two jobs and did not have enough time to spend with her children. She wanted to make enough money selling real estate to get back to her family.

Now I was able to tell her the Specific Benefits she would receive from my class. I gave her a Specific Promise: You take my class and you will be able to do a better job closing, which means you will be able to get more people to make the decision to buy right now, and therefore you will make more money. As a result of this, you will be able to quit your old job quicker and get back to spending more time with your children.

She eagerly joined the class. It may have been different if I had not determined what Specific Benefits she wanted. Without them, all I could have promised her in return for the time and money the class would cost her was that she would be able to do a better job closing. It would have been a tough sale because she would have had to decide if being able to do a better job closing would be worth $500 and thirty hours of her time.

With the knowledge of the Specific Benefits she wanted, I promised her that she could do a better job closing, get more people to buy now, and make more money. Not only that, but it would allow her to quit her old job quicker so she wouldn't have to work two jobs. Then she would be able to spend more time with her children. It was much easier for her to justify spending $500 and thirty hours of her time to accomplish all of that.

She could achieve all those logical benefits by doing a better job closing. There is no way I could have guessed what benefits she wanted, so it would not have made any sense to assume what she wanted. But it was so easy to ask.

If I had just assumed what she wanted to achieve from doing a better job closing and promised her a bunch of benefits that she did not want, it would cause objections and would not motivate her to buy. The benefits we promise people must be those that are important to them.

In a previous class there was another woman who also had as a Primary Interest the ability to do a better job closing. She too had children but was not interested in being able to spend more time with them. She wanted to be able to buy better clothes, go more places, and have a good time while she was still young.

How much do you feel she would be motivated if I told her that she could make more money so she could spend more time with her children? What if I promised the woman who wanted to spend more time with her family that she could buy better clothes, go more places, and have a good time while she was still young? If I had not determined the Specific Benefits each of them wanted, I would not have made either sale, and neither of them would have received the benefits they wanted.

Blowing the sale is exactly what salespeople do when they promise their prospects benefits without first finding out what is important to them. That is what Bob did when he told me the benefits that I would get from buying his car.

Tips on Finding the Specific Benefits

In order to determine the Specific Benefits our prospects want, all we have to do is ask why their Primary Interest is important to them. Then ask the same question in a little different way: How would that benefit you? Then follow it up with what comes naturally: Why is that important? How would that help you? Why is that something you would want?

Do not sound like a cop grilling a suspect; be genuinely interested in what they want and what is important to them. Prospects will appreciate your interest and they will help you discover how to solve their problems. That will result in more sales and better sales.

Of course before we can ask, "Why would that be important to you?" we have to know what it is that our product does that is important to them (their Primary Interest). Then we can ask the questions to determine the Specific Benefits that are important to them. From then on, everything we say is based on what is important to the customer.

When asking the six Feeling-Finding questions, we are looking for the Primary Interest. Part of this process is asking, "Why is that important to you?" That gives us the Specific Benefits. When we ask the other Feeling-Finding questions, "What do you dislike most about your previous experience?" and "Why is that a problem for you?" we get a preview of possible objections. We also know what not to talk about so we do not cause objections, something that is a common problem in most sales presentations.

If we wish, we can continue the line of questioning about what they disliked most about their previous experience and why that was a problem for them. By doing so, they will tell all of the negative benefits or bad experiences they had that they do not want to receive again.

Sometimes a problem arises when continuing the line of questioning about dislikes. Prospects sometimes end up reliving the bad experiences they had before, which causes them to end up in a bad mood. Rather than have them relive the bad experiences, my choice is to put them in a good mood by being able to picture the great benefits they will receive after buying my seminar.

The Un-Specific Benefits

In selling a sales seminar or class, I determine the prospect's Primary Interest. In the process of determining the Specific Benefits prospects want, I invariably ask the important question, "If you could achieve that Primary Interest, how would that benefit you?" Then I get the answer, "More sales." I then ask, "Why would that be important to you?" Most of the time the reply is, "We would make more money." That is not specific; that's general.

From these two answers I have learned absolutely nothing. Everybody wants more sales and more money from sales training. I must ask, "Why would it be important for you to earn more money?" Many times I get strange looks from this question, but I always get an answer that helps make the sale. Without more information I have the same sales presentation as every other trainer in the world. "You take my class and you will make more sales and more money." That does not sell training.

If prospects indicate that it is a rather dumb question, I tell them, "Some people want to buy a new boat, others want to put it away for retirement, others want to take a trip to foreign countries." Then I ask the question again, "Why would it be important for you to earn more money?" Then they understand the reason for the question and they answer it. I make sure I do not make them feel dumb when I do this. The approach to use is, "Sorry, I did not ask the question the right way."

Remember the two women earlier in the chapter who each wanted more sales and more money. One of them wanted to be able to do so in order to quit her second job and spend more time with her children. The other wanted to do so in order to buy new clothes, go more places, and have a good time while still young. The specific reasons they wanted to make more money were very important to them, and therefore to us.

Making money is not the only un-specific benefit for people who take sales training, but in almost all sales presentations involving purchasing agents, managers, owners, trainers, sole proprietors, partners, and corporate officers, whether in business or industry. They all want to make more money from just about every purchase they make from every product or service on the market. If we do not know why it is important for them to make more money, "we don't know nothing." At least, nothing of value in selling.

Another un-specific benefit that gives no information is when the prospect states the same benefit in different language. I have asked hundreds of prospects why it would be important for them to have more life insurance. At least a hundred of them answered, "So I would have more protection." Another hundred answered, "So I would have more coverage." Because I learned absolutely nothing, I must ask again, "Why would it be important for you to have more coverage?" Then I discover what is important to them, and therefore an important part of making a sale that is Customer Driven.

Ask purchasing agents why it would be important to increase production without increasing costs and they will usually answer, "Because we would make more money." I cannot ask them why it would be important to the company to make more money, because that is the reason the company is in business, to make money. What I can say is, "You do not own the company, so why would it be important to you if the company made more money?" Then I get a great answer, which takes us to Chapter 8, The Dominant Buying Motive.

CHAPTER 8

THE DOMINANT BUYING MOTIVE

T he dictionary states that "Dominant" means superior or ruling. Remember, "Dominant" is the one that rules, no matter how strong others may be. "Motive" is defined as causing to act, causing motion.

The word "Automotive" means self-moving. Originally, the word itself did not tell what the product was, but only that it moved itself. In selling, the Dominant Buying Motive does not relate to the product, but only to the person who is moved to buy the product. What this means is that just because prospects believe you have a good product, suitable for them and worth the money, they will not buy unless they feel within themselves a reason to move.

So the Dominant Buying Motive, the DBM, is in the person, not the product, and the one thing that will cause people to buy; not get them to like it, not get them to need it, but *cause them to act on it*. It does not cause them just to make a decision but *to do it, to buy*. This is what makes the sale Customer Driven. It means there is no need to be a pushy salesperson.

The Desire Step is one of the five steps of selling, except that it is not a separate step in itself. Desire is built through the entire sales presentation. During the discussion of the feelings of the prospect, it grows until we get to the DBM. Here, first the prospect, and then the salesperson discuss this emotion. Then we promise to satisfy that emotional need. That is how Desire is built.

Most books on selling that I have read state that it is important to determine the Dominant Buying Motive. That is nice, but just realizing that the DBM is important is not enough. We must understand why it is so important, we must know how to discover it, and we must then discover it if we want to build desire to buy. People do not buy products simply because they are good products that are worth the money. People must have a desire to buy.

Desire Out of the Past

One couple bought another home before selling the home they lived in. For more than a year, they made payments on both. Why? The combination living-dining room with the fireplace looked just like the one in the house of the wife's childhood in southern Indiana. The emotion was such she had to buy now.

Gene said he wanted a ranch home. I asked him, "Why?" and he said he did not know why. I asked him where he grew up, and he said it was on a farm. I asked him what kind of home he had on the farm, expecting him to say a ranch style. No! He grew up in a two-story frame house. I asked him if he liked it, and he said, "No. I hated it." I asked, "Why?" He said that he was an only child, and every night he had to go upstairs to bed. I asked why that was a problem. He said, "I was cut off from the rest of my family. I can still remember sitting on the floor all alone, peering through the bannister rails, wishing I were downstairs with the rest of the family."

Although both of these people had childhood memories that would determine the type of houses they would buy, it is probable that neither of them realized that when they began looking for a home. Once the emotion is stated, the salesperson hears it. But more important, the prospect relives the emotion. We must determine the prospect's DBM and let the prospect relive the feeling. In reality, we do not motivate our prospects; *they motivate themselves.*

Vicki was selling high-quality hand-crafted gifts, and one of them was a bunny rabbit that wholesaled for twenty dollars. She showed it to a buyer for a gift shop. The buyer held one of the bunnies and remarked that twenty dollars was too much money. She said, "That's pricey, that's pricey." She then held the bunny up close to her bosom, hugged it, and whispered, "I'll take four of them."

I was talking to a young man about life insurance. I asked why it was important to him, and he replied that he did not want his children to go hungry if he died. I told him they wouldn't go hungry, that they would get Social Security and that there were places they could get food.

The young man became very serious, and said, "My father died when I was a boy. We had food, but it was cheap food. We had clothes, but they were hand-me-downs. And we had toys, but they were what someone else didn't want." This young man not only motivated himself to buy, but he motivated me to make sure he had enough insurance so he would never put his children through what he had gone through.

Do you think the feeling was strong? It stayed with him for twenty years, and the story has stayed with me for another twenty-five years.

Desire for Today's Reasons

Many texts state that the DBM is related to the product. For instance, a common misconception is that the dominant motivation to buy life insurance is love of family. It is sometimes, but not always so. Joe Manson bought life insurance to protect his family because he loves them. I asked him why it was important to him to have the protection, and he said, "Because I love them," while pointing over his shoulder at pictures of his wife and children. His DBM was love.

Charles wanted to take care of his family until the children were twenty-one. He said it was his obligation. It is almost like paying taxes. He doesn't love them, but will take care of them because it is a debt he *feels* he has to pay. (By the way, what does this prospect think of his wife? Does he care what happens to her after the children are grown?)

I told a man that his partner had purchased $200,000 of life insurance. He asked me, "How much would $200,000 be on me?" His DBM was the desire to keep up with his partner.

Another man said he wanted life insurance so that when he died, people would not point to his grave and call him an S.O.B. because he didn't take care of his family. His DBM was not wanting to be criticized after death.

One day I received a call from the husband of a client whom I had not convinced to buy life insurance. Now he wanted to talk about insurance. I set the appointment and asked him why he was calling now. He said, "I turned fifty this weekend." When you turn fifty, you will know what he meant.

Same product, different Dominant Buying Motives. The motivation is in the person, not the product. It is not selling people on the importance of life insurance; it is selling them on *doing something* about it. To do that, we must discover their feelings and emotions.

How to Motivate Buyers

If we wish to motivate people to buy, we had better quit wishing and find out what emotion will motivate them to buy!

Someone can say, "Yes, it is emotional to want to take care of your children, your wife, your husband, but it is also logical." True, but it is not the logic that motivated these buyers. *Emotion is dominant over logic in motivation.*

There is a very large roller coaster at Cedar Point, Ohio, and I know that it is absolutely safe to ride. I will not ride it. I do not *feel* safe. My *feeling* of fear keeps me off, even though my logic says it is OK to ride it.

I understand we have ten times the chance to win a million dollars in the lottery than to be killed in the crash of a scheduled airliner. Those are logical statistics that don't sway a "white-knuckle flier." Emotion rules.

I have claustrophobia. Now, you convince me to get in a box and let you close the lid. Convince me. No, my emotion will not allow it, no matter how much logic you use.

Grady McKay, while training salespeople to sell the Dale Carnegie Sales Course, said it this way: "What is put into the mind by emotion cannot be removed by logic."

One last thought on Emotion. Remove the E, and you get Motion. If we want to get Motion from prospects, discover their Emotions and let them discover them along with you.

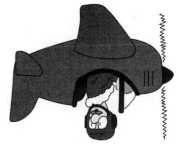

Nobody has to remind the "white-knuckle flier" of the fear of flying, and nobody need remind me that I have claustrophobia. No one has to discover our fears for us. In *sales*, many times we discover the prospect's DBM and, at the same time, enable the prospect to dis-cover it. At other times we discover what the prospect already knew, and the prospect simply relives it. Either way, we have to initiate the discovery.

How to Discover the Dominant Buying Motive

To discover does not mean to invent or build. To discover means that it was already there and all we did was locate it and see it for the first time. Just like Christopher Columbus.

Now comes the easy part, how to discover the prospect's DBM. All we have to do is ask "Why?" The trouble is, ask "Why" to what? Getting the DBM is the next step after getting something else. The "something else" we have to do first is determine the prospect's Primary Interest. The Primary Interest is *what* benefit the prospect wants from our product. The DBM is *why* they want that *what*.

In talking with Linda Chavez, who leases and sells commercial real estate for Eyde Company, she stated that her Primary Interest in a sales class was to be able to motivate people better. The Specific Benefits she wanted were to be able to eliminate put-offs and make more money. I asked her why that was important to her and she replied, "Phil, I don't know; I just always like to be the best. Always!" That always wanting to be the best is the feeling that caused her to join the class.

One person whose name I will not mention is a very capable and successful real estate agent who generally sells new construction. Her Primary Interest was to motivate people to do it now. The Specific Benefits she wanted were to have more time for herself and make more income. Looking for an emotion for her DBM, I asked her why that was so important to her. She gave me another Specific Benefit, that she wanted to do more for her children.

As I still did not arrive at an emotion or feeling, I said, "You make lots of money already, why do you want to make even more?" After a moment's hesitation she replied, "When I was divorced three years ago, I had never worked for a living, because my husband did not want me to work for money. All of a sudden I had to support myself, and I have done well. Last year my ex-husband reported income of $51,000. I want to make more than $51,000."

Then I had her DBM and the sale. It was no longer a decision to come up with $500 for a sales class. It was a decision to come up with $500 to better motivate people so she could make more money and be able to do more for her children. As if that were not enough, it would give her a chance to make more money than her ex-husband did. She joined the class and made more than $51,000.

The Examples of Banquet Catering and Dominant Buying Motives

Problem: It took too long to serve the dinner. Some were finished while others were just starting. They blamed me.
Primary Interest: Serve the food quickly so people eat together.
Dominant Buying Motive: *I want people to know I did a good job.*

Problem: The food was cold, and people complained to me. I was embarrassed.
Primary Interest: Food served hot.
Dominant Buying Motive: *I don't want to be embarrassed.*

Problem: They did not serve when they were supposed to, and I had to spend much of my time in the kitchen, when I should have been with the guests. I did not enjoy myself.
Primary Interest: Food served on time.
Dominant Buying Motive: *I want to be able to enjoy myself.*

Problem: They ran out of silverware, and some of the guests had to eat with spoons. My daughter was not proud of the reception.
Primary Interest: Enough silverware to go around.
Dominant Buying Motive: *I want my daughter to be proud* of her wedding reception.

Years ago when I sold banquet catering, I called on an association across from the State Capitol building. The woman in charge of the catering said they were not interested in changing caterers. She agreed to answer some questions, and I discovered she had a problem. The governor came to banquets there, and three times in a row, he had exactly the same menu. He asked the woman in charge if that was all she ever served there. I asked why that was a problem for her, and she replied, "I was so embarrassed. The governor chewed me out for something over which I had no control."

Her Primary Interest was simply to make sure the governor did not get the same meal three times in a row. Her Dominant Buying Motive was *wanting to eliminate the embarrassment* of being chewed out by the governor. My Specific Promise was: "Let me handle your banquets, and I will make sure the governor, or other important guests, don't get the same meal two or three times in a row. That way you will never have to suffer the embarrassment of being chewed out like that again."

I ended up with the business even though, at the beginning, she said she was not interested in changing caterers. This amounted to about fifty banquets per year. Incidentally, she did not even ask our prices. What I really did right was to ask, "Why was that a problem for you?"

Remember that the DBM is the desire to gain some feeling or emotion, or to eliminate some feeling or emotion. This means that we can either mentally take the prospect into the future to experience a good feeling, or take the prospect into the past to relive a bad experience.

For example: In the sale of catering to the association, we went into the past, letting the woman relive the bad experience with the governor. I asked, "Why was that a problem for you?" Her DBM was to eliminate the bad feeling (to eliminate the embarrassment).

In the four examples listed about banquet catering, three of the DBMs are going into the future to gain a good feeling: "I want people to know I did a good job," "I want to be able to enjoy myself," and "I want my daughter to be proud." In the other example the DBM is to eliminate a bad feeling from the past: "I don't want to be embarrassed."

Which way we should go depends on the circumstances. If the prospect had a bad experience in the past, we could ask, *"Why was that a problem?"* We continue asking until we find the bad emotion or feeling they want to eliminate, then promise to eliminate that feeling in our Specific Promise. Again, I feel it is better to take them into the bright future rather than away from the dark past.

If the prospect is looking toward something good in the future, we should ask, *"Assume we can do this good thing you want in the future; what would that do for you?"* We continue asking until we reach a feeling and in our Specific Promise tell them we can help them gain that good feeling.

Either way, we should only promise what we can deliver. In each of these examples from selling catering, I could and did help those prospects achieve their Primary Interests and Dominant Buying Motives. The promise to help them achieve their PI and DBM is called the **Specific Promise**.

Purchasing Agents

A Special Case: Many people say that purchasing agents buy from logic rather than emotion. Let's ask Shelly Cooper. Shelly was a senior at Michigan State University who left school for three months to work in the purchasing department of a large manufacturing plant. There she assisted the purchasing agent in buying small tools. After she had been there two months, the purchasing agent went on vacation, leaving Shelly to do the buying.

Assume a salesperson comes into the office while Shelly is buying and demonstrates a tool superior to what the plant is using but for the same cost. Logic says to buy it. But Shelly knows the present supplier is a friend of the purchasing agent and the purchasing agent will evaluate her work and give her a recommendation when she returns to school.

Does Shelly opt for self-preservation and continue buying from the present salesperson who is a friend of the purchasing agent? Or perhaps, with a sense of pride, does she do what would be better for the company and buy the better tools? Either way, her decision is based on emotion: self-preservation or pride.

(AUTHOR'S NOTE: While writing this book, I saw Shelly and put the question to her to see which way she would have handled it. Before she could answer, her fiancé, Pat, said, "She would buy the new product because that would be the right thing to do." With pride, Shelly said, "He's right." Strictly emotion.)

What if the purchasing agent did not go on vacation and he was faced with the same decision? Why would the PA purchase the better product? Would it be pride, self-preservation to keep the job, or a desire to impress the boss? Perhaps he would stay with the present purveyor due to friendship with the salesperson and not rock the boat. These are all some form of emotion and could become the Dominant Buying Motive.

Spartan Motors produces chassis for fire trucks, motor homes, and other specialty vehicles to the tune of $200 million annually. Lynn Brehm, Director of Purchasing, attributes much of the company's growth to better communications in purchasing.

In the April 1995 edition of *NAPM Insights*, the official publication of the National Association of Purchasing Management, he states, "I meet almost daily with the director of operations and keep in touch with our four plant managers regularly." He is obviously proud of the company's success and states, "There is less finger-pointing and a better acceptance by all departments when we achieve goals." Pride is a great motivation to buy what is best for manufacturing.

In some companies, those who use the materials and tools are included in the purchasing decision, while in others, they have no say. Factories do not have emotions, but purchasing agents do, and they are the ones who make the decisions. When selling to purchasing agents, we should talk about the logical benefit for the end user, and about the emotional benefit that will be achieved by the purchasing agent who makes the decision. We will sell more because we are selling both the steak and the sizzle: the logic and the emotion (The Primary Interest and the Dominant Buying Motive).

Purchasing agents are everywhere

All purchasing agents do not have the title. There are all sorts of people who act as purchasing agents for others. Human resources directors make purchasing decisions, as do managers, sales managers, and even owners. That's right, owners buy tools, materials, and supplies that others use.

Those who made the decisions in the banquet catering examples were all acting as purchasing agents for a bunch of people who would use the service. The ultimate consumers would not even see what was purchased until weeks or months after the decision to buy was made. Some of those decisions were made exclusively on the basis of buyers' emotions. Read them! They all said, "*I* want," or, "*I* don't want."

Mothers and fathers do quite a bit of purchasing for use by others. They make the decisions to buy insurance, investments, homes, automobiles, food, or other commodities that are used by the entire family. When buying, they must take into consideration the needs of the family members and may have to answer to them, but ultimately the decision is made by the buyer for his or her reasons. Salespeople must address the needs of both, parents and family members.

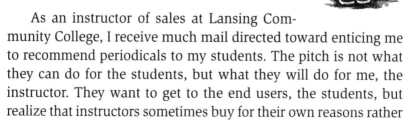

I remember that when I was a child buying my mother a present, I usually got her something that I liked. After I grew up, I didn't change. For Valentine's Day, I would make sure that the box of candy I bought for my wife contained chocolate-covered caramels. They were the square ones. I still purchase things for other people for my own reasons.

As an instructor of sales at Lansing Community College, I receive much mail directed toward enticing me to recommend periodicals to my students. The pitch is not what they can do for the students, but what they will do for me, the instructor. They want to get to the end users, the students, but realize that instructors sometimes buy for their own reasons rather than for the benefit of the students. It is similar with purchasing agents; sometimes they buy for their own reasons rather than for the benefit of the end users.

No matter what we sell and to whom we sell, many of our prospects are acting as purchasing agents. We had better remember that and discover the Dominant Buying Motive of the buyer we are talking to.

Why Salespeople Do Not Discover the Dominant Buying Motive

1. They do not know how. They do not realize that all we have to do is determine the prospect's Primary Interest and then ask why that is important or why is that a problem. They do not realize we must continue asking that question until the response is a feeling or an emotion. That feeling or emotion is the Dominant Buying Motive.

2. Some salespeople feel they are prying unnecessarily into the prospect's business. They do not realize our job in selling is to satisfy emotional needs as well as logical needs. The emotional needs of people are just as important as, if not more important than, the logical. The thrills or hurts from emotions last long after the logic is forgotten. We can only satisfy those needs if we know what they are.

3. Others feel that asking these personal questions makes the prospect momentarily uncomfortable. This is true, the same as when a doctor asks personal questions of a patient. But if we don't ask these questions, we may base our solution to the problem on inadequate information. Then everyone will be uncomfortable more than momentarily.

4. Here is a real problem. It is uncomfortable for us to ask the question, "Why is that important to you," or "Why is that a problem for you?" We seem to think the answer is obvious, and that the prospect will think we are dumb for asking. Re-

member, prospects have their own emotions that will cause them to move. That is what we seek. Ask and you shall receive.

5. Here is the biggest problem. We do not know the track or the questions verbatim. In order to get the right information and become effective, we must know the track so well that there is no fear and no fumbling. If you have acting experience, you know the feeling of confidence and professionalism that comes from knowing your lines well.

If we know the questions verbatim, we do not have to be thinking what we will ask next; therefore, we can listen intently to the answers the prospect gives us. If we are thinking what we will ask next, we simply cannot listen effectively. This means that in order to become effective in discovering the DBM, we have to practice and practice.

A visitor to New York asked a musician, "How do I get to Carnegie Hall?" The answer: "Practice, man, practice."

Here is our track so far:

- Attention Step

- Indicator (Optional)

- General Interest Statement

- Bridge to Information

- Info

    — Fact-Finding Questions

    — Feeling-Finding Questions

CHAPTER 9

THE SPECIFIC PROMISE

I n the Info, we determine the Primary Interest (the logical benefit that the prospect wants from our product), the Specific Benefits that the Primary Interest will give the prospect, and we discover the Dominant Buying Motive (the emotional reason why the prospect wants those benefits).

Now we give a **Specific Promise**.

A promise is difficult to define but easy to understand, therefore a definition is unnecessary. Little children know what a promise is, and grown-ups do also. Nations use promises in trade agreements and treaties which are accepted as law. In business, a promise is  taken so seriously that it is a contract. A promise by both parties binds husband and wife together for life.

The point of all of this is that promises are taken seriously by just about everyone. When you promise people something, generally they will believe you. Advertise your product, market your product, sell your product, and most people know it really won't do what you say. Make a promise that it will do something and they will believe you.

When was the last time you had a salesperson promise you that a product would perform? It does not happen often. Salespeople may exaggerate and stretch the truth a little, but when it comes to making a promise, they tend to take it a little more seriously. And, so does the listener.

In a sales presentation, when we know that we can deliver the benefits the customer wants, we should make a promise that we can do just that. We should take it seriously, and the customer will do so also. In order to be meaningful to the customer, the promise must be specific to what that person wants. If it is not something he or she wants, it will be meaningless.

Use Their Exact Words

In the Customer-Driven Track, if we have done the Info properly, we will know exactly what prospects want to get from our product, as well as the exact benefits they want to derive from it. We know this exactly because we listen to their exact words.

Exact words are important to prospects, and therefore to us. Many experts suggest paraphrasing their words, but doing so changes the meaning in their minds. We don't want to do that, because the mind is where the sale takes place.

While working in a class on understanding the DBM, I was questioning a young salesperson about why he wanted to do a better job selling. His Primary Interest (PI) was to develop a better Customer-Driven Track. The Specific Benefits he wanted were standard: make more sales, make more money, and do more things for his family. After more questioning, suddenly his face lit up as if he had made a discovery. He said, "Do you know what I want? I want to leave a legacy."

Another class member responded, "His DBM is to break sales records." The young salesperson shook his head from side to side and said, "No! I want to leave a legacy." I said, "You want to leave a legacy, right?" He replied, "Yes, I do."

I used his exact words and they were the right words. He knew what he meant when he said legacy, while the rest of us could only guess. But, we did not have to guess, because we could use his exact words. Remember, by not using exact words, the other class member brought on an objection.

In the Specific Promise, use your prospects' own words to promise to deliver to them the PI they want, the benefits they said were important to them, and the DBM they wish to satisfy. This way you won't be the cause of an objection.

In selling a sales class to a young lady, I discovered that her PI was that she wanted *more confidence in selling* radio time. I asked why that was important, and she said it would help her *make more sales, and therefore, more money*. I asked her why that was important to her, and she told me that she wanted to *buy things for her family, to repay them for all they had done for her.*

My Specific Promise was, "You take this class and you will develop *more confidence in selling* radio time. As a result you will *make more sales, and therefore, more money.* Then you will be able to *buy things for your family to repay them for all they have done for you.*"

The Specific Promise is a promise to deliver *what* the prospects want from our product, *for the reasons* they want that benefit. We promise only what we can deliver, and we do not promise more than they say they want.

For instance: I knew that this young lady would gain more confidence in selling radio time, so I could promise that. She indicated to me that more *confidence in selling* would result in *more sales, and therefore more money*, and that she would use it to *buy things for her family to repay her family for all they have done for her.* Therefore I could assure her that she would gain those benefits. I could not tell her that she would see more people, or that she would be number one in sales, or anything else she did not mention. Notice, I used her exact words as much as possible in the Specific Promise.

The Specific Promise does not start with the word "if." It generally starts with "you." You buy my product and you will get (nothing more and nothing less than the prospect wants). Sometimes it starts with "I," as in, "I will (whatever our promise is)."

Remember, do not talk yourself out of a sale by promising what the prospect does not want. Talk in terms of the other person's interest, because people buy for their reasons, not ours. Make it Customer-Driven.

After giving a Specific Promise we "Trial Close" or use successive "Trial Closes." If the answers are favorable, then "Close" right away without giving any facts or benefits about the product. The Specific Promise is so powerful and effective that much of the time it is the conclusion of the presentation. Trial Closes will tell if this is true.

In other words, eliminate the Conviction Step if the prospect does not require it. We do not want to bore the prospect with unnecessary information. We do not want to "buy the product back" after the prospect has mentally bought it from us.

We will discuss the Conviction Step in Chapter 14. We discuss Trial Closes and Closes later in this chapter.

Continuing the Examples of Banquet Catering

Problem: It took too long to serve the dinner. Some were finished while others were just starting. They blamed me.
Primary Interest: Serve the food quickly so people can eat together.
Dominant Buying Motive: I want people to know I did a good job.
Specific Promise: You let my company serve the dinner, and we will do it quickly. All the people will be able to eat together and they will know you did a good job.

Problem: The food was cold, and people complained to me. I felt embarrassed.
Primary Interest: Food served hot.
Dominant Buying Motive: I do not want to feel embarrassed.
Specific Promise: You use my company to serve your dinner, and the food will be served hot. That way people will not complain to you, and you need not feel embarrassed.

100

Problem: They did not serve when they were supposed to, and I had to spend much of my time in the kitchen, when I should have been with the guests. I did not enjoy myself.
Primary Interest: Serve when they are supposed to.
Dominant Buying Motive: I want to enjoy myself.
Specific Promise: We will serve when we are supposed to, and you will not have to spend time in the kitchen. You can spend it with your guests and enjoy yourself.

Problem: They ran out of silverware, and some of the guests had to eat with spoons. My daughter was not proud of the reception.
Primary Interest: Enough silverware to go around.
Dominant Buying Motive: I want my daughter to be proud of her reception.
Specific Promise: I will make sure we do not run out of silverware, so none of the guests have to eat with spoons. That way your daughter can be proud of her reception.

What about Third-Party Interests?

A friend of mine asked me to talk to his two daughters, to convince them to start putting money away for retirement using whole life insurance. He had not done that early enough for himself. During the Info, they both indicated an interest in whole life insurance. Their interest in whole life insurance was not for retirement, but so they could use it to borrow money to buy a home later in life.

In my Specific Promise, I told each of them that they could use the insurance to buy a home later in life. I did not mention using it for retirement, because neither of them mentioned that as a benefit they wanted.

Our Specific Promise must be in the interest of the buyer. In this case the father did get his daughters to buy, but for their reasons, not his.

There are occasions when we talk in terms of the buyer, plus a third party. Purchasing agents sometimes purchase a product for what it will do for the company, while at the same time making the decision for an emotional reason. Here we mention both in the Specific Promise.

"You buy this new widget, and you will find that it will decrease production time with no increase in cost. That way you will get the recognition from the operations department that you want."

Again, just as in the example of the friend's two daughters, we talk in terms of the buyer's interest. We do not mention any benefit unless the buyer has mentioned it as being important. Here the buyer mentioned both the benefit for the operations department, and the personal benefit. So both of them are included in the Specific Promise.

Time to Close?

Immediately after giving the prospect the Specific Promise, there is an excellent opportunity to close the sale. For this reason, we will briefly discuss Trial Closes and Closes now. They will be covered in depth in a later chapter.

Remember that a sale takes place in the mind of the prospect. Let's go back to the young lady who was considering a sales class. She said she wanted more confidence in selling radio time, so she could make more sales and, therefore, more money. She wanted to be able to buy more things for her family, and her DBM was to repay them for all they had done for her.

My Specific Promise was: "You take this class and you will develop more confidence in selling radio time. As a result, you will make more sales, and therefore, more money. Then you will be able to buy things for your family, to repay them for all they have done for you."

I then asked, "*How does that sound?*" She said, "Great!" because that was exactly what she said she wanted. I then asked *if that would be worth an investment of five hundred dollars,* and she said, "Yes." Then I asked *if getting that would be worth thirty hours of her time*. She answered in the affirmative on each of these three opinion-finding questions, because she had mentally decided to join the class. Those three questions are Trial Closes.

A Trial Close is not *trying to close*; it is finding out what the prospect is thinking. If she thinks that sounds great, that it would be worth an investment of five hundred dollars, and that it would be worth thirty hours of her time, she probably is ready to buy. In this particular Close, I did not ask her "*if*" she wanted to buy, because in the Trial Closes she already indicated she was ready to buy. I just showed her how to sign up for the class, and she did.

The time to ask for the order is when the prospect is ready to buy. We determine when the prospect is ready to buy by using Trial Closes. The three Trial Closes I used with this young lady told me that mentally she wanted the benefits of the class and was willing to pay the price in money and in time. For me to keep on talking about the class would serve no purpose. If she had any further questions, she would ask them.

Recall the woman in the last chapter in charge of catering for the association. She was embarrassed when the governor questioned getting the same menu three times in a row. My Specific Promise was, "Let me handle your banquets and I will make sure the governor or other important guests don't get the same meal two or three times in a row, and that way you will not have to suffer the embarrassment of being chewed out like that again."

I then trial closed with something like, "How does that sound?" She asked when we could start, without asking any other questions. She did not ask about our capabilities, our equipment, or even our prices. She had a problem that I could solve. That was all she needed to know. Why should I keep talking when someone is ready to buy? The Trial Close let me know when to stop selling and close the sale.

When we give the prospect the Specific Promise, we should immediately Trial Close. If our prospects are ready to buy, we should then Close. If they are not ready to buy, they will tell us where they are in the sale, and we can proceed based on what they say.

CHAPTER 10

THE MENU

Wouldn't it be nice if prospects told you what aspect of your products turn them on, and what the benefits are that they want you to talk about, even though they may not be familiar with the products? Wouldn't it be great if getting that information were as easy as reading a restaurant menu?

What if you knew that after you made your presentation, you could ask, "How does that sound?" and hear your prospect say, "That is just what I want." Wouldn't that be great?

Not only is that possible, but it is easy to achieve; and so simple that you may wonder why you never thought of it. Try it, and you will wonder why it is not standard practice.

I can take a multiple choice test from just about any course and pass it without being familiar with the course or attending even one session. But if I had to take the test without the advantage of multiple choice, I would be in trouble. Students love multiple choice because it is so easy. There are only four choices from which to choose, and one of them is always the right answer. Teachers love multiple choice because of its simplicity and exactness.

The designers of computers saw the possibilities of using multiple choice questions in their programming. It made operation of the computer so simple that even computer illiterates like me have the ability to operate one and appear to be an expert. I not only appear that way, but when I can use a series of multiple choice questions, I am an expert. On a computer it is called a menu, a term borrowed from the restaurant industry.

In sales we can use the same type of menu with its simplicity and exactness to get information even when our prospects are not familiar with what we can do for them. Prospects and salespeople both like using the menu because it is simple, exact, and user friendly for both parties. It achieves the goal of both salesperson and prospect; it pinpoints prospects' problems that salespeople can solve with their products. As in a multiple choice test, it always contains the right answer.

Do you ever have difficulty trying to determine the biggest problem your prospects have that you can solve with your products? With the menu system, all you have to do is lay out four choices and ask the prospects to choose the one that is their biggest problem. They will tell you. It is that simple.

Do you have difficulty determining the exact benefits your prospects will achieve from using your product? With this menu system, all you have to do is ask why they chose that particular problem, and how they will benefit from solving it. They will tell you. It is that simple.

The concept is simple and using the menu is simple. The most complicated part is explaining the system in its entirety in one chapter. To make it easier to understand, we will use the analogy of a restaurant menu. Once a restaurant menu is produced, it is easy to use. The only real complexity of a menu lies in designing one that tells customers or clients what you serve.

The Restaurant Menu

Figure 1 is a type of menu that is generally standard in the restaurant industry: easy to read and understand. Regardless of

ENTREES

BEEF

Prime Rib — simply the best.
The best cut 21.95 Regular 18.95 Petite 15.95

Kansas City Strip — chargrilled with the bone,
complemented with herbed burgandy mushrooms 15.95

The T-Bone — 22oz of the finest available, chargrilled
and complemented with fried onion shreds 17.95

Filet Mignon — only from the center, chargrilled to
your specifications, served atop a garlic crouton, complemented with bernaise sauce 10oz 17.95 6oz 12.95

SEAFOOD

Peppered Potato Crusted Salmon — garnished
with tomato basil butter sauce 13.95

Blackened Northern Whitefish — served with a
Cajun jambalaya 12.95

Steamed Crablegs Maryland Style — complemented with a lemon herbed butter sauce 14.95

PORK & LAMB

Chargrilled Boneless Pork Chops — crowned with
a peach, apricot, and apple glaze 12.95

Salt Roasted Herbed Lamb Loin — served atop a
port wine, spring vegetable glaze, accented with a
roasted shallot yogurt 14.95

· · · · · · · ·

Figure 1.

whether customers are familiar with the items on the menu, they can quickly choose what they want. It is such a simple and effective concept that it would be difficult to come up with a method that works better for the restaurant or the customers.

Assume that you go to a restaurant that has no menu. They serve the entrees you see on Figure 1. The server comes to the table and tells you about all the items they serve. Minutes later you would remember very little about what was said, and you would be bored from hearing about all the items. That certainly would not be effective.

To get away from having to read an entire menu, the server could assume what you want to eat and just tell you about that item. If the item does not appeal to you, the server could go to the next item, and the next until something sparked your interest. Of course that wouldn't work very well either.

The server could find out what you want by just asking what you want to eat. The problem here is that by not knowing what is on the menu, you would not know what is available. Maybe the server could ask probing questions, such as, "Are you a seafood lover?" or, "Are you still into red meat, or do you prefer fowl?" That might be a fun game, somewhat like *Twenty Questions*. But you don't go to restaurants to play games.

I have it! The restaurant could show a video which would either present everything the restaurant serves or just those items they think you would be interested in. Maybe they could use one of these notebooks that open up like a stand, with lots of glossy pictures in it. The waiter could show you that with a short commentary about each item, and watch closely for buying signals, hoping to notice when you see something you like.

That's all pretty silly, isn't it? None of those methods could replace the simple menu that informs customers what is available so they can make a choice.

If it is true that it would be silly to use such ineffective methods to determine a customer's needs, why then is it that salespeople use those methods to determine prospects' needs? That is exactly what many of them do.

Salespeople either give a verbal presentation about their company or their products that bores most prospects; assume what the prospects want and just talk about that; make suggestions on a trial and error basis; or show a short video that may have nothing to do with what the client wants. Some simply ask probing questions hoping to hit the correct response.

Why Not Use a Menu for Sales?

On a computer, the most complicated programs can be made simple and effective by using a series of menus. The same applies in a restaurant. A typical restaurant menu will allow the server to find out exactly what customers want, what they want to accompany the main course, how they want it prepared, and what condiments they want to spice it up.

Using a menu in sales can be just as simple as doing so in a restaurant. It allows the salesperson to determine exactly what prospects want, how they want it prepared, what they may want to accompany it, and how to spice it up so you can sell the sizzle along with the steak.

No matter what the product or service, a menu can be a simple and effective tool to determine what prospects want and what benefits they want us to talk about. This is important because if we talk about what interests them, they will listen. If what we talk about does not interest them, they will tune us out and we risk talking them out of buying, even though our product may be right for them.

There are times when we cannot find our prospect's Primary Interest simply by asking the Standard Feeling-Finding questions. Perhaps the prospect is not familiar with our product or has no experience on which to base answers. Perhaps the prospect has no knowledge of the product we are selling. Yet we must discover what we can do to solve a problem for prospects before they will buy from us.

An example would be like the situation Todd Stehouwer finds every time he makes a call. Todd has a unique software program specially designed for machine shops. Most of the personnel he calls on have never heard of his product. They don't know such a program exists. They don't realize he can make their jobs easier, improve the quality of their work, and save them both time and money.

In a situation like that, just asking what they like or dislike most about their current or previous program would not produce the information necessary to discover a problem that Todd might be able to solve.

Also, there are times when, for some other reason, it may be necessary to continue searching for the prospect's Primary Interest even after asking the Standard Feeling-Finding questions. That is especially true in more creative or sophisticated selling.

We cannot just start telling prospects what our product will do for them, and how it is going to solve their problems, until we find out what it is that they want done.

In Customer-Driven Sales, we must first determine what our prospects' needs are before we tell them how we can fulfill those needs.

The same type of menu that is used in a restaurant can be used in sales to determine our prospects' needs and what aspect of our product will best fulfill those needs, even if they never heard of our product before. They will also tell us exactly what benefits they want to achieve by using this product that they never heard of.

Anatomy of a restaurant menu

One of the first things you will notice about the menu in Figure 1 is that you have the advantage of using the sense of sight. You can look at different choices until you determine what you want. When using a written menu in sales, our prospects also have the advantage of using the sense of sight. This makes it easier to get the proper information from prospects, and the prospects themselves realize and appreciate this.

We get more and better information because prospects can discuss the choices while reading the menu. They cannot do that while listening to a salesperson. Think about how complicated it would be to determine what you want if you went into a restaurant that had no menu.

It does not matter that you are unfamiliar with what a restaurant serves, because of the menu. The breakdown on the menu is between Beef, Seafood, Pork and Lamb, and so forth. You choose Beef, which takes you to the next submenu.

Here you find the Kansas City Strip Steak. There follows an explanation of how it is served: chargrilled with the bone. Then some salesmanship: complemented with herbed burgundy mushrooms.

A server you have never seen before comes to your table and, without any sales presentation, quickly determines exactly what you want to eat from the items featured. The server never approaches the table wondering how to determine what you want, a problem that constantly confronts salespeople.

All the server has to do is ask you what you chose and listen to your answers. The server can then repeat what you selected to determine if that is exactly what you want. Obviously you will say, "Yes," because you were the one who made the decision of what you wanted from the menu.

The restaurant menu describes only those items it serves, and gives enough descriptive information on each item to ensure the customer can understand what is offered. It is simple, effective, and exact for both customer and server. It creates no resistance and little fear of rejection.

The Sales Menu

In sales we can design a menu for any product in the world that will do the same thing. With it we can give simple, effective, and exact descriptive information to let the prospect understand what we offer. And there will be no resistance or rejection.

People do not buy our products. They buy their perception of the benefits they will receive from what we sell. Therefore our menu is not made up of products or services but the benefits that others derive from using our products or services. Just like in a restaurant menu, it does not matter whether anyone else offers the same thing. We can offer benefits that are the same as our competitors or benefits that they do not offer. The purpose of the menu is to help prospects and us to determine what they want so we know what to talk about.

By using a menu in sales, we need not wonder whether we are offering prospects exactly what they want, because they will tell us by their selection. We and the prospects will be on the same track, and we will both know that what they order will fit their needs. We recommend exactly what they told us was important to them, for the exact reasons they stated, and let them make the decision to buy. They end up buying what they said they wanted for the reasons they said were important to them.

Another positive aspect of letting the prospect choose the benefits of our products is that it eliminates many objections. Most objections are the result of salespeople talking about what they have no business talking about or not mentioning what they should have. When we let the prospect determine what we talk about in our presentation, there is little to object to. Using a menu reduces the number of objections.

A restaurant menu shows only those items that it serves; therefore, no matter what the customer chooses, the restaurant can furnish it. Our sales menu only shows those benefits that we can deliver. As a result, no matter what the customer chooses, it is something we can do. We control this, because we make up our menu.

Usually customers do not realize what benefits they will derive from a product or service until after it is bought and paid for. You don't know much about your new home until you have lived in it for a while; you don't realize what you have in a new car until you have driven it for a while; you don't realize the real benefits of any product when buying it, only those perceived benefits. Those perceived benefits are controlled by the salesperson. Those perceived benefits comprise the choices on the menu.

A Menu for Software

Let's look at the menu Stehouwer uses for his software sales and see how it works. It is very simple. Like most sales menus it has only four items, all benefits, the solutions to the major problems that machine shops face (see Figure 2).

First, the menu is not similar to a brochure or chart showing the major features of our product or service. It shows the solutions to the prospect's problems. It is closely related to the multiple choice menu of a computer program, containing the minimum number of words possible. Those few words are inscribed on separate plastic tags as shown in Figure 2 so they can be moved around or realigned by the prospect. Following each written Tag is a verbal portion of the menu which tells the specifics of the Tag and tells the benefits of the Tag.

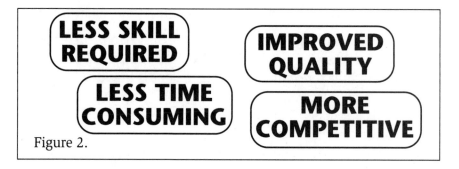

Figure 2.

When Stehouwer uses his menu containing the solutions to the problems that machine shops generally have, those who receive the presentation get the chance to tell him which problem they want solved. Different shops have different problems, but they generally fall into the same four categories: Requiring so much skill to do the work, quality control, taking too much time to do the job, or beating the competition. Every shop owner or manager would like to solve problems in at least of one of these areas. Therefore the Tags consist of the solutions to those problems:

Less Skill Required	Improved Quality	Less Time Consuming	More Competitive

The Tag, *Less Skill Required*, is the only written portion of the first benefit. This is followed by the verbal portion, first the specifics of the Tag, and then the benefit of the Tag. For instance: *One of the reasons machine shops like our program is because it takes less skill to set up the program as well as to do the actual machining. This reduces the reliance on highly skilled machinists and reduces labor costs.*

The next Tag, *Improved Quality*, is then explained: *Many shops like our program because they turn out a better quality product within closer tolerance. This reduces the need for rework. That, in turn, helps profitability.*

With the *Less Time Consuming* Tag: *Some appreciate the fact that the program takes less time to set up and less time to put into production. This is important because it means employees have more time to do other important jobs. Again, that enhances profitability.*

With the last Tag, *More Competitive*: *Many of our clients like the fact that they become more competitive in the industry. This gives them a better chance to pick up business that would otherwise go to another shop.*

Notice that the word "you" does not appear in this menu. The purpose of a menu is not to tell prospects that they will receive these benefits. The purpose is not to sell but to gather information. This is important, because if Stehouwer tells them that they will like all the benefits of his software, they may not believe him. It is believable that others like different benefits of his product.

Tell how others have benefited. Prospects will believe that some other shops became more competitive by using this program but may not believe that it will make their shop more competitive. Stehouwer wants his prospects to believe everything he says. If they do, he has a better chance of making a sale.

After he states the verbal portion of the menu, Stehouwer lays the Tags in front of the prospect and asks that prospect to choose the one that would be most important. "Of these major benefits, which would be most important to you, *Less Skill Required, Improved Quality, Less Time Consuming* or *More Competitive?*" The prospects will always choose the one that is right for them.

By making a choice, the prospect has said, "This is the benefit that is of Primary Interest to me, and it is what I want you to talk about. I either don't have a big problem with the others, or this one is the key to more success for me and my shop. This is my Primary Interest."

This takes Stehouwer's prospects out of the "should I buy or should I not buy mode" and involves them in conversation where they tell him which of the benefits he can offer will be the most helpful for their business. When that is accomplished, no matter which Tag they have chosen, they begin to talk about how his product will benefit them.

Thereafter, Stehouwer talks only about what the prospect has chosen as a Primary Interest. If prospects want to hear more about the other three benefits, they will ask. They already know he has the other benefits because he just told them how others liked those benefits.

Sometimes the First Sale Is You

In Stehouwer's case the menu is based on benefits of his product. That is because the product is all he sells, and it is so different than other software. In other forms of selling, the first sale, and therefore the first menu, is composed of the benefits of working with the salesperson, rather than the product. A second menu tells the benefits of the product or service. Some menus are a combination of benefits of product and salesperson.

Jennifer Nelson Mefford sells radio space. She uses the following Benefit Tags: *Product Knowledge, Service, Listening,* and *Creativity.* Notice that they do not mention radio. Her first job in selling a new account is not to determine what type of advertising to use, but to get the prospect to say, "I want you to help us with our advertising needs." It really would not make too much sense to be talking about the type and number of ads to use if the business went to somebody else.

Before she attempts to get prospects to choose the proper amount or type of advertising copy, she must get them to make the decision to advertise with her station, and specifically with her. That is her job. Companies are going to advertise; she does not have to sell them on that. She has to sell them on doing their advertising with her.

After she has sold them on letting her solve their advertising problems, she can set out to determine what problems she can solve with her radio ads.

Even in the restaurant business, there is a sale that takes place before customers ever see the restaurant menu. The first decision is: which restaurant to patronize. People actually see a menu in their minds, the choice of restaurants to go to, before they see the menu in the restaurant.

Assume that you have just finished a tough week. It is Friday afternoon and you decide that you would like to go out to eat. You call your spouse and say, "How would you like to take it easy tonight and dine out?" Your spouse says, "Great. What restaurant were you thinking of?"

116

First you have to decide where you want to go. What is your Primary Interest in a restaurant? Do you want to go to some place that is *Close*, so you don't have to spend much time driving there after your long day? Or is your Primary Interest going to a place that has music and a *Relaxing Atmosphere*, so you can make it a special evening out, where the two of you can be alone together?

Sometimes it is more important to chose a restaurant that has *Ethnic Food* that you have been dreaming about for the past couple of days. Or, this may be one of those times when you want to go to a place where your *Friends Hang Out* so you can socialize.

Notice that in choosing a restaurant, the choice of being *Close*, having a *Relaxing Atmosphere*, *Ethnic Foods*, or being where *Friends Hang Out* is made by the diners before the restaurant ever has a chance to sell its selections. Notice that none of these four choices had anything to do with price, quality of food, or service.

If you choose a restaurant that is *Close*, it does not mean that you are not interested in *Ethnic Foods*, a *Relaxing Atmosphere*, or a place where *Friends Hang Out*; it just means that being *Close* is your Primary Interest.

The first sale to be made in the restaurant business is getting people to come to a particular restaurant. After they get you there, then they have another menu to determine what you want to eat.

Often it is the same in sales. The first sale is getting prospects to accept you as their agent or supplier. After you get them to accept you, there is another menu to determine what they want in your product or service.

Those who wish to advertise can do so through radio, TV, newspaper, other periodicals, or many other methods. Jennifer Nelson Mefford's job is not to talk them out of using other mediums, but to sell them on the fact that she is the person who can help them become more successful. She can do this by solving the problems they wish to solve after she has discovered what problems they wish to solve. She can best learn this information by using a menu of Tags.

Menu Tags

By using the Tags, Jennifer gets her prospects to compare the different benefits she can give them. She is comparing what she can do with what she can do, rather than what she can do versus what the competition can do.

After they accept her as their account rep, she has another menu to determine what they want from her service. The second menu is incorporated in her written information gathering form, not with Tags.

In Customer-Driven Sales, many times we must first get our prospects to know that we are the right provider, the right salesperson, the right company, or the right restaurant to solve their needs; not their product needs, but their individual needs, their logic and their feelings. In effect, we must determine what problems they want solved, rather than what they want in our product or service.

The problems people generally have with those who sell advertising is that some salespeople have a limited knowledge about how to use their product. Many advertisers have provided inferior service in the past or have untrained salespeople who did not listen. There are also salespeople who lack the creativity so necessary in selling advertising.

From this information, Jennifer determined her Tags: *Product Knowledge, Service, Listening,* and *Creativity.* After using those Tags to get her prospects to believe she can solve their problems with radio, she then designs their programs to help them get what they want for their advertising dollar.

In designing programs, those who sell radio space realize that people who advertise their firms on radio do not all want to derive the same benefits. Therefore, after clients have made the decision to use her services, Jennifer has another menu in her written questionnaire to gather information. That menu includes these benefits:

Some business want to stress the *Image* they want to portray. Others want to achieve more *Name Recognition* so people will think of them first when they have a need. Then there are those businesses that simply want to *Increase Traffic* to increase sales. Yet others wish to let the public know about *Special Promotions* they may be running.

Her clients then tell Jennifer what they wish to achieve. Therefore, she knows how to set up their ad campaigns in partnership with them.

When You Are the Product

In many forms of selling, the salesperson's first job is not to sell prospects on using a specific product or service but to get them to buy it through this particular salesperson. In this case, the salesperson is the first product to be sold.

If I were selling life insurance, my job would not be to convince the prospect to buy life insurance but to convince that person to buy life insurance from me. I can sell someone on putting together a great insurance program; but what if they buy from another agent?

Often selling insurance is like pulling teeth. The prospects hate it, but do so only because it is a "necessary evil." If I first sell prospects on working with me, they become partners in the planning. The net result is better for both of us.

Every real estate agent has had the experience of working with clients who, all of a sudden, buy through another agent. That is not the fault of the buyers. Some agents simply do not sell their prospects on buying through them. Eliminate that problem by first selling them on the idea that you will be their partner in finding them a home.

Have you ever had the experience of selling someone on a piece of equipment or an idea, only to have the prospect make the purchase from a competitor? Solve that problem by first selling prospects on buying from you. Then you work with your clients on helping them get what they need.

In selling, your job is not to convince people to buy the product you sell but to convince them to buy it through you. To do so you must first convince prospects that they are talking to the right person or company to solve their problems. To do this you must know what their problems are, and how they will benefit from solving those problems. Then you must convey that message to the prospects. That is Customer-Driven Selling.

CHAPTER 11
CREATE YOUR OWN MENU

Every product has certain features that do things people are interested in, and most salespeople tell their prospects about those features. A menu is not designed to talk about features; it is designed to find out what benefits prospects want that our products can give them. People do not care about our product features unless those features provide benefits or solve their problems.

We have no business telling prospects that our product or service will do something for them unless we know of a benefit they will receive or a problem it will solve. To build a menu we must first determine what problems our customers want solved or benefits they seek to gain.

I was working with a convention bureau that sells groups on having conventions in a fairly small city. One of the services they provide to attract groups is having a *Liaison Person* assigned to remain with the conventioneers during their stay in the city. That is nice because there is always someone close at hand to answer questions about the host city. The sales force really stresses this point in their sales presentation, as they should.

Stephen Moore, Vice President of Sales and Marketing for the convention bureau, helped me create a menu with the purpose of selling the idea to the sales force. It included the following Tags along with the one that said, *Liaison Person*:

- *Accessibility*: *In the center of the country and in the center of the state, the city is easy to get to on the freeways that converge from every direction. There is excellent airline access from an airport only ten minutes from downtown.*

- *Small City Advantages*: *Easy to get around; many hotels, fine restaurants, museums, and shopping centers within walking distance from the convention center; lower crime rate than major cities which means conventioneers feel safe walking around.*

I displayed the three Tags, *Liaison Person*, *Accessibility*, and *Small City Advantages*, and asked the salespeople to choose the one they felt was most important. To my surprise, they all chose to have a *Liaison Person*. They all felt this major benefit was most important to groups looking at their town.

I told them I had just returned from a convention in a large city within the state. One of the salespeople interrupted me and said, "I would not go there to a convention." I asked, "Why not?" She said, "There is too much crime there. I wouldn't feel safe." Another said, "I would not want to go there either, because it is too large and too difficult to get around."

I asked them, "How come you all chose *Liaison Person* before, and now you say something else is more important?" They both said, "We don't have to worry about those problems in our city."

The point is that those who make the decision which city will host their conventions do have to worry about those problems. When I asked the same question of the sales staff again, "Which of these would be most important to you?" they were about equally divided among *Liaison People*, *Accessibility*, and *Small City Advantages*.

A Menu to Solve People Problems

While in the life insurance business for over twenty years, I asked prospects what they disliked most about life insurance. Interestingly enough, none of the three answers that dominated the list were characteristics of the life insurance itself.

The three were: "I do not trust agents," "I do not understand insurance," and, "I do not know if what I have is what I should have." These are the problems that life insurance prospects generally want solved.

Sometimes there will be only three Tags in a menu, as was the case in the convention bureau and in the selling of life insurance. My three Tags in the life insurance business were as follows:

Trust in Agent   **Understand**   **Based on Goals**

The verbal portion of my menu went like this:

- *One of the reasons people like to work with me is because they find they have an agent they can **Trust**. I tell the truth, and this is important because most people are not experts in insurance, and they need someone they can trust.*

- *Many people I work with find that they can **Understand** their insurance. I put it in simple language that is easily understood. That means they do not have to guess anymore. They know what they have, what it will do, and what changes to make if necessary.*

- *Then there are those who are happy because they see they can have a program **Based on their Goals**, where everything is organized to do what they want done. After all, that is why they buy it, to do what they want done.*

This menu consists of the solutions to the problems that people generally have in deciding to buy life insurance.

Another way to determine your menu is to determine what reasons cause people to enjoy working with you. An example would be Deb Kinney of Re/Max Home Professionals. Her menu consists of:

Trust   **Listen**   **Knowledge**   **Service**

The verbal portion of Deb's menu:

* *One of the reasons people like to work with me is because they can **Trust** me. I am honest with them in every situation. That way they don't have to worry about whether or not I am telling the truth, so they can concentrate on finding the right home.*

* *Others like the fact that I **Listen** to them. I find out what is important to them, and that is what I look for in a home. That way they end up with the home that fits them, rather than what someone wants to sell them.*

* *There are those who appreciate my **Knowledge** about the real estate business, what is available, the in's and out's of financing and how to complete the transaction with few problems. If there is something I don't know, I find out.*

* *And then there are those who like my **Service**. I am there when they need me. I am easy to reach and answer calls quickly. Usually I am only as far away as the phone.*

The Combination Menu

Some menus are a combination of benefits of the salesperson, the company, and the product. An example is Michelle Carpenter of Core Electronics. Here is the menu she uses to sell their specialized software program:

Trust   **Consultant**   **Easy to Use**   **Reliable Service**

* *One of the reasons companies like our product is because they realize that our presentation is entirely honest. We generate **Trust** by making no exaggerated claims. This is important because the most expensive software is that which does not do the job.*

- *Others like our product because we act as a **Consultant** during and after the sale. We help our clients make the original decision to buy and help them in the use after purchase. This makes it easier to put to use.*

- *Another reason companies like the product is because it is **Easy to Use**. Sometimes personnel tell us, "I have to train every person to use this software." They appreciate the ease of training people to use our products.*

- *Then there are those who appreciate our **Service**. The software is a quality product, but when there is a problem, we are there to help solve the problem. This is important because it eliminates down time for them.*

Notice that the Tags *Trust* and *Consultant* apply to the salesperson, *Reliable Service* pertains to the company, while *Easy to Use* pertains to the software itself. In selling some specialized equipment or services, part of the menu pertains to the company or the salesperson, while other parts pertain to the product.

In the sale of insurance, real estate, securities, and many other products, the first sale is the agent him/herself, because the products are quite similar and most of them can do the same job. There are also forms of selling where the entire menu consists of product benefits.

A Product Menu

While teaching a class of salespeople, I gave them a menu that could be used in the sale of automobile tires:

- *Some people are primarily interested in **Safety**. They want to make sure that the tires they have will perform well during emergencies. This is important to them to ensure their own safety as well as the safety of their families.*

- *Others are interested in **Performance**. They want tires that are true in tracking at high speeds and on corners.*

- *There are those who want tires that are **Smooth Riding**. That way they are not bothered by the unwanted noise or vibrations.*

- *And then there are some who just want to make sure they have **Good-Looking** tires. They feel that tires are an important part of the beauty of their automobiles.*

I then asked how many would be primarily interested in safety. Seven of them raised their hands. One of them said that safety was important to him because many times his family rode with him and he wanted it to be safe.

There was an engineer in the class, who along with four others stated that performance was most important. He said that when he cornered at high speed, he wanted tires to give him some warning that they were going to break away from the pavement, rather than doing so all at once.

About four or five class members stated that the most important benefit they would look for in a tire was that it be smooth riding and free of unwanted noises or vibrations.

A couple of the young people in the class said that the most important thing they would look for was looks. I asked one young woman why the looks of her tires were so important to her, as she would not see them while driving. She said, "I can't see them, but the guy behind me can."

If you were selling tires, what would the proper sales presentation be to each of these people? I am sure that if you were to talk to the one interested in safety for his family, that you would not stress your tires' good looks.

In talking to one of the people who wanted to get away from annoying noise and vibration, you would not talk about keeping the tires from breaking away without any warning.

If I were to sell tires on what is important to me, no matter what my Primary Interest, I would miss three-fourths of my prospects' interests. Even if I used a presentation based on all of the benefits, I would be boring them 75 percent of the time with information not important to them.

Designing the Menu

First figure out what the Primary Benefits are that people want in your product, regardless of whether you have these benefits exclusively or if others also have them. The purpose is not to show why you are better than the competition but to gather information better than the competition.

These benefits may be benefits that prospects derive from you if yours is a product or service where you must sell them on buying from you. It may be a combination of benefits of buying from you and the product. Look at some of the examples in this chapter in order to relate to your menu.

Listen to what people say are the biggest problems customers have with salespeople in the same business as you.

Talk to present clients and ask them what they most like about buying from you and ask them what they would want you to do even better. The solutions to these problems can become your menu Tags.

Have a stamp or sign shop make up some plastic Tags, one inch by three inches, with a key word or words to describe each of the benefits on your menu. Make them in different colors, beveled on the back so they are easy to pick up on a flat surface, and with rounded corners so they do not poke you or the prospect (see figure 2, page 113).

Write the verbal portion of the menu that tells the specifics of each benefit and the importance of each benefit. Memorize these words verbatim so you can say them in your sleep. That way you can say them smoothly and be able to listen to your prospects and hear what they say. You cannot listen to them if you are thinking about what you are going to say next.

Using the Tags

When giving the Menu to your prospects it is best to go through the Tags in a chronological order that makes sense. On Deb Kinney's real estate menu, her Tags go from *Trust*, which has to be first, to *Listen* to gather information, to *Knowledge* of the market and financing, to *Service*.

Then memorize the questions you will ask when you lay the Tags out:

1. *Which of these major benefits would be most important to you?* (Summarize them.)
2. *Why did you choose that one?* (They are giving you their Primary Interest, what they like most about what you are selling.)
3. *Why would that be important to you?* (They tell you the benefits they want so you know what benefits you should talk about later.)
4. *How would that benefit you?* (They tell you about more benefits they want. Here you are looking for the Dominant Buying Motive.)

Notice that the word "you" appears in each of these questions. That is because the "you" is the person who is about to make the decision based on a perception of the benefits to be gained.

What is happening here? Your prospects are telling you the good things about your product. They are telling you the benefits that they will receive so you do not have to guess, grope, or probe. They will tell you exactly what the benefits are that you can give them and how to motivate them to buy.

Once the prospects have told you what it is they like about your product, and the benefits they would derive from it, you can make them a Specific Promise that you can do those things for them. Remember, you made up the menu and you only included those things you could do, so no matter which Tag they choose, you can furnish it.

Again, remember that if you do not have to be thinking about what you are going to ask next, it becomes easy to listen to what the prospects are saying. You can watch the prospects for buying signals. You can tell how interested they are in what you are selling. You can remember all the benefits they want.

Another interesting aspect of using the Tags is what can be learned by watching the prospects' involvement with them. There are times when prospects will pick up one and shake it or hold on to it tightly. This usually indicates they attach great importance to that particular one and you have hit a strong nerve. Other times they will nonchalantly or in an offhand manner barely touch one with the end of a finger. This would indicate either a reluctance to say, "This is what I need," or they are not really enthusiastic about the choice. In this case, you probably will have to work for the sale. But you know where they stand.

The next thing to do is practice on present customers to get a good feel for using the menu, and also so you will realize how well interactive selling is accepted by clients. A benefit is that they will like you better for showing an interest in them. This will cement your relationship.

Optional method of using the Tags

If you are talking to an important client and you want to make sure you do everything exactly right, use the entire track, including Attention, General Interest, Bridge to Info, Fact-Finding Questions, Standard Feeling-Finding Questions, and then the Menu. After asking for the Specific Benefits the prospect wants, give a Specific Promise. Then Trial Close. (Simply ask, "How does that sound?")

If you are having trouble getting the Attention or Interest of a particular client, simply lay the Tags down in front of him or her. The client will ask, "What are those?" Then you say, "Those are the different benefits others get from my product," and go into the menu.

Steve Marietta is a Sales Engineer for Akemi Plastics. He worked on the molds that form the aluminum skin on a new jet airliner. The president of this company wanted Steve to be able to sell other accounts, so Steve was sent to a class in selling.

As Steve went through the class, he found that the Tags made an excellent Attention Getter. On his first sales presentation to a company in Ohio, the purchasing agent sat reading a paper and told Steve, "Tell me what you have." Steve says he dropped the four Tags on top of the PA's paper. The PA looked up and said, "What are these?"

Steve told him that they were the benefits that other companies received from dealing with Akemi Plastics, and went right through the Menu. The PA chose a Primary Interest, and Steve made his first sale ever, on his first call ever.

Bob Baxter, Director of Marketing for Multicom, producer of videos for business, industry, and government, says that many times he has used the Tags as an Attention Getter by just dropping them in front of his prospects. He says that the prospects invariably ask, "What are those?" They are asking for a presentation, so Bob gives them one. He says that this method grabs their Attention and carries him right into the sales presentation with him in control.

While I was checking with him on the wording of this last paragraph, he told me that he had just finished a presentation where he used the Tags as an Attention Getter. He was meeting with the management of a consulting firm that was about to make its first promotional video. Bob had talked with them about producing the video but had not nailed down the business.

He said that he met the three of them for lunch. While they were just engaged in informal conversation he casually dropped his four Tags on the table and continued with the informal talk. After a couple of minutes, they could not stand it any longer, and one of them asked, "What are those?" When Bob explained those were the reasons other companies liked having him do their work, they all listened to what he had to say. Before the lunch was over he had a commitment to do the work.

One Product, 5 People, 5 Different Presentations

I called on a company to enroll some of their salespeople in a class that uses the menu for determining customer needs. I first had to sell the human resources director, then the branch manager of one of their seven branches, and then three salespeople.

The following is the menu I used for this presentation:

• *Some people develop* **More Self-Confidence** *from the class; not "I can," or " I will," but the kind of confidence where they know they are good. This added confidence is transmitted to their prospects and helps increase sales.*

• *Others like the* **Selling Skills***; they learn how to get prospects to want to hear about what they are selling, how to handle objections, and how to close more effectively. This is where they develop the basics of selling and put those basics into practice.*

• *Some salespeople find out how to do a better job of* **Motivating People** *to buy now. By doing so, they eliminate a lot of No's and Put-Offs, get less rejections and more sales. If prospects do not buy now, they may never buy, or they may buy from somebody else later.*

• *Then there are some who like the fact that they learn more about* **Customer-Driven Sales***. They are able to get their prospects to give them the information they need to solve problems rather than just sell a product. This way the salespeople know how to talk in terms of the customers' needs. The result: long-term customers rather than a quick sale.*

First I covered the Menu with the human resources director who had to make the decision on whether the company would sponsor the course for its sales force.

She chose *Customer-Driven* as her Primary Interest. I asked why she chose that benefit, and she stated that by selling based on the customers' needs, the company could pick up lifetime customers rather than making a onetime sale. When I asked why that was important, she stated, "We are a fast growing company, and we need the repeat sales in order to continue this dynamic growth."

I then agreed with her that this would be great for the company and inquired how this increase in sales and growth would benefit her. She said, "I want to be part of the dynamic growth that this company is achieving."

Then I made a Specific Promise, "You get your salespeople in this class, and they will develop the ability to sell based on customers' needs. As a result they will pick up more lifetime customers, which will give you the repeat sales that your company needs to continue the fast growth. That way you can be part of the dynamic growth that your company is achieving."

I asked, "How does that sound?" She said that was exactly what she wanted. She then called a branch manager to ask him to talk to me to see what he thought.

When I met with the branch manager, I put him on the same track with the same Menu. He chose *Selling Skills* as the most important to him. I asked him why he chose that one and he said that his salespeople never had a class in the basics of selling.

I asked why it would be important for his salespeople to develop the basics of selling. He responded that they then could sell more and make more money for themselves and the company. I asked why that would be important to him, and he said that would let him do other important things while I trained his salespeople. Again I asked why that would be important to him. He told me that I would do the work and he would get the rewards.

I made a Specific Promise to him that I could give them a class in the basics of selling so they could make more money for themselves and the company. That way he could do more important things while I trained his salespeople. I would do the work and he could get the rewards.

The branch manager said that was exactly what he wanted and set up a meeting for me with his salespeople.

Notice that what I told the branch manager about the class was completely different from what I told the human resources director. Each promise was completely true and exactly what each wanted from the class. That is the reason they both bought the idea with enthusiasm.

I talked to his three salespeople and they all joined. The reason they all joined was that I found their individual Primary Interests and Dominant Buying Motives, the same as I had with the human resources director and the branch manager. One of them chose *Self-Confidence*, another *Selling Skills,* and the others *Motivating People*. They each received a different promise based on what they wanted from the class and the benefits they would gain. They also bought the idea with enthusiasm.

The Information Getting was the same with all five of the people involved in this one sale. Because I received different information from each one, I tailored a different sales presentation to each one. They each bought for their own reasons. I did not have to guess or probe or wonder because I knew they would tell me what they wanted. Then all I had to do was promise they would achieve what they wanted. They all received the benefits they sought.

I did not have to worry about whether or not I could fulfill my promise, because I gave them a choice of what was on my menu. I received no objections because I only promised what it was they told me they wanted. It was easy for them and it was easy for me too.

There is no simpler, more effective, or profitable way to sell than this. Prospects will tell you what aspect of your products turn them on, what benefits they want you to talk about, even when they are not familiar with the product. It is as easy as reading a restaurant menu.

Not only that, but after you make your presentation, you can ask, "How does that sound?" and have your prospect say, "That is just what I want." It is so simple that you may wonder why you never thought of it. Try it, and you will probably make it standard practice for gathering information.

CHAPTER 12

HANDLING OBJECTIONS

Under ordinary circumstances, the Specific Promise is the end of the track. Up to this point, we have determined the path of the presentation. The prospect may have determined what we talked about through the information we gathered, but we followed the path of Attention, General Interest, Fact Finding, Feeling Finding, the Menu, Specific Promise, and Trial Close.

Take the Path Determined by the Prospect

After giving the Specific Promise, generally we should Trial Close with something like, "How does that sound?"

- If the prospect says, "great," probably we should close.

- If the prospect says, "OK," probably we should Trial Close again.

- If the prospect says, "how are you going to do that?", we should go into the Conviction Step. Then Trial Close again.

- If the prospect says, "it sounds good but I do not believe it," we should offer evidence. Then Trial Close again.

- If the prospect asks a question, we should answer it. Then Trial Close again.

- If the prospect states an objection, we should handle the objection. Then Trial Close again.

It seems there are a lot of Trial Closes listed above. That is because from this point on, it is time to find out if the prospect is ready to make a decision. The prospect will tell us what stands in the way of making a decision. We handle whatever stands in the way, and Trial Close again to see if we answered the prospect's question or problem. If the Trial Close indicates that we have done so, we close.

Many times an Objection will surface at this point.

The answer to an Objection must be simple, honest, easy to understand, in good taste, and must keep the salesperson and the prospect walking arm in arm toward the common objective, a sale that is beneficial to both parties.

In a sales presentation, we do not have the luxury of being able to classify an Objection by type, choose and use a proper method of answering it from the list of seven choices, while at the same time remaining tuned to what the prospect is saying. Even if we could do all that, 90 percent of the Objections we get could still be answered best by one method: Feel, Felt, Found.

Stamp Out Buts

When she was in elementary school, my daughter, Jenny, complained about her homework. She said, "Dad, math is really tough." That I do remember. What I do not remember is how I answered that objection. I probably told her something like, "No, it's not. You just have to learn how to do it," or, "Yes, but you have to learn it to graduate." Either way, it was the wrong thing for me to say.

If I had known how to handle Objections properly, I would have said, "I understand how you Feel. I sometimes Felt the same way when I was your age. What I Found was that the more I learned about math, the easier it got. You would like to have it become easier for you, wouldn't you?"

What is wrong with the answer, "No, it's not, you just have to learn how to do it"? Well for starters, I alienate her by telling her she is wrong. Then I tell her it is her fault. We are not walking arm in arm toward our common objective. She was looking for help, and I let her down. You have just seen the "Direct Denial" technique, one of the seven methods of handling Objections. Please do not use it.

What is wrong with the "Indirect Denial" technique, another method? That is where I say, "Yes, but you have to learn it to graduate." The infamous "Yes, but" technique. When I say, "Yes, but," I put up a barrier to walking arm in arm toward a common objective. I am talking out of both sides of my mouth.

> Your wife seems to be nice, but …

> Your son is intelligent, but…

> I don't mean to interrupt you, but…

Some authorities recommend the word "however" instead.

> Your wife seems to be nice, however…

> Your son is intelligent, however…

> I don't mean to interrupt you, however…

I don't mean to alienate you, but… . I just told you that I don't mean to alienate you. As soon as I say "but," you better brace yourself, because I am about to alienate you. I am building resistance when I should be reducing it.

I was talking about this in one of my classes and a young lady named Trina just had to tell her story. She said, "I used to hate it when my mother did that to me. She would tell me something I did was all right and add a loud 'but… .' " Trina said, "I hated that, I hated that."

Assume you are a prospect for a sales class, and after the Specific Promise, you say the price is too high. If I say, "Yes, the price is high, but... ,", you had better brace yourself because I am going to tell you why the price is not too high. That makes no sense, saying the price is high and then telling you why it is not. Again we are not walking arm in arm toward the common objective. When we use the "Yes, but" technique, we are inviting a conditioned response.

What is a conditioned response? A conditioned response is when we are responsible for the response we get.

So many people have used the same phrase before, that the response is predictable.

A prospective customer walks into a showroom. The salesperson comes up and says, "May I help you?" The conditioned response is, "No thank you, I am just looking." That is not the response we want, but we really ask for it when we say, "May I help you?"

Why use "Yes, but" if that is going to get us a response we do not want? Why ask for resistance? There is a more honest, easier-to-understand method, which is in good taste and which will help us continue walking arm in arm toward the common objective, the sale: Feel, Felt, Found.

Feel, Felt, Found

Same scenario: I am making a presentation to you on a sales class. After the Specific Promise, you tell me the price is too high. "I understand how you Feel. The price is high. When I took the class, I Felt the same way. I went ahead with it and Found that the increase in sales from what I learned paid for the class. It also increased my income by 20 percent the next year. You would like to increase your sales by 20 percent, wouldn't you?"

Or I could say, "I understand how you Feel. Roger Bebee of Kabe Realty Felt the same way. He took the class and Found that it made selling easier and helped him build his own company later on. How would something like that sound to you?" (This would be particularly appropriate if the prospect had indicated the desire to build his own company later on.)

I could also say, "I understand how you Feel. Others have Felt the same way. What they Found was that they increased their sales and income. You would like to be able to increase your sales and income too, wouldn't you?"

The first part is Feel. I understand how you Feel. Here we want prospects to know that we really do understand how they feel. That helps us continue with them arm in arm. We do not want to use a *but* or a *however*, as those words build resistance. We want to stay by the prospect's side. We also want them to know they are not alone in feeling that way, so we present evidence that we know others who Felt the same way or that we Felt the same way.

All of this talk about feelings is called a *cushion*, because we want to cushion our prospects from any hurt, harm, or confrontation. The cushion has to be there because for all their lives as prospects they have been subjected to inept answers to their Objections, so they are bracing themselves. Now they find that we, as salespeople, are really on their side. Because of that, prospects are more receptive to what we suggest. What we suggest is always beneficial to them, because we discovered what they wanted in the Info.

- FEEL: A cushion to let the prospect know we understand.
- FELT: Evidence that the prospect is not alone in what he or she says.
- FOUND: A benefit to the prospect for going ahead with the purchase.

An interesting aspect to using Feel, Felt, Found is that we are talking about our mistakes or other people's mistakes, not the prospect's. With the "Yes, but" technique, we are telling the prospect why his or her thinking is off and ours is correct. With Feel, Felt, Found we are admitting that we made the mistake, and we tell how we corrected it, or how others made the mistake and how they corrected it. We end with the benefit that was received from correcting the mistake. Then we Trial Close.

Feel, Felt, Found are not just words to be said. If you do not understand how the prospect feels, ask until you do. Prospects know if you really do understand or if you are just saying the words. You learn so much when you ask, and you will feel more professional when you do so.

Someone once told me that when we handle an Objection we should not hit the prospect over the head with our answer. We want to Trial Close, not gloat. That automatically puts us back on the track arm in arm. When we say, "You would like to be able to do that, wouldn't you?" we are again talking in the prospect's interest. At the same time, we get an idea if the answer was sufficient, or if it is time to close.

Exceptions to Feel, Felt, Found

If we do not understand the reason for the Objection, or if we are not sure it is an Objection that we should answer, or if we suspect it is not a real Objection, we can ask, "Why do you say that?" or "Would you please repeat that?" Sometimes prospects will clarify the Objection, and sometimes they will answer it themselves or dismiss it.

Sometimes we should not answer an Objection but just cushion it. Many times people will give offhand Objections they really do not mean to be answered. If a prospect says something like, "Insurance companies don't want people to understand their policies," we should just say, "I understand how you Feel." Sometimes people just like to vent their feelings. We should let them do so.

Sometimes we should just cushion the Objection with, "I understand how you Feel," knowing that we will be covering the Objection later in the presentation when it will not put us in disagreement. For instance, if someone in a presentation says, "All whole life insurance is basically the same. When you die, they don't give back your cash values," I would just cushion the Objection at the time. Later on, when making my recommendations, I would say, "One of the reasons I am recommending this particular policy is that when you die, your family doesn't get just the face amount of the insurance, but also the cash values."

Sometimes an Objection is unanswerable, and we just have to admit that fact. When I bought my present car, it did not come with automatic speed control. The salesperson admitted it, but I still bought the car. When we make a purchase, many times we do so in spite of Objections we may have. Others do, too! Sometimes, we have to admit that we cannot overcome the prospect's Objection, knowing that we will lose the sale. If a prospect for life insurance had a heart attack last week, there is nothing I can do about it. *We do not have to answer every Objection.*

Often we know beforehand what Objections are going to be brought up. We can anticipate them and answer them prior to the time they are spoken by the prospect. If we were selling a home without a fireplace to someone who really wanted a fireplace, we could mention that one of the strong points of this home is that, "You can choose where you want the fireplace. Not only that, but the price of the home takes into consideration that it has no fireplace. This means you save money on the price of the home and also gain the opportunity to choose the location and style of the fireplace you would like. That's a nice benefit, isn't it?"

Remember, in the Info, we ask our prospects what they dislike about their present or previous product. They tell us the Objections that may come up later, unless we answer them ahead of time. We have a chance to answer them in the Conviction Step of our presentation before they surface as Objections, and before the Close.

As far as I know, there is only one problem with using the Feel, Felt, Found formula. We have to work at getting used to it because most of us are in the habit of saying, "Yes, but." Like any other time we set out to improve our selling skills, we have to consciously work to overcome the old habit and replace it with a new habit. If you have trouble doing this, I will understand how you feel. I felt the same way.

Price

Four friends of mine have something in common. One sells insurance, one sells homes, one sells cars, and the other sells sound systems. They all say that people buy on price. They say that if they do not have the lowest price, they do not get the sale. That is so strange because the rest of my friends do not own the cheapest cars, the least expensive homes, the lowest cost sound systems, nor the cheapest insurance. Who are the people my friends are selling to?

Somebody once told me that price is not an Objection. I agree with that to a certain extent. When I ask prospects what they dislike most about their insurance, many times they will answer, "Paying for it." I automatically say, "Other than paying for it?" Then they will usually give me the answer I want.

The first problem with the answer, "Paying for it" is that it is not answering the question I asked. I still do not know what it is that they dislike most about their insurance. I want to know what Objections they have to insurance that I can solve for them.

"Paying for it" is what I dislike about everything I own: my home, my car, my insurance, my clothes, my food. "Paying for it" may be an Objection, but it is not a dislike about what I am selling. I think my home, my car, my insurance, my clothes, and my food are all too expensive. That is not an Objection to any of those things. "Paying for it" is a smoke screen that covers up the real Objections people have.

I do not have the money to buy a new home, a new car, more insurance, or the clothes I want. If I wrecked my car and had to buy another, I would find the money to buy a new one. It would not be the least expensive one, either. If I need a new suit to attend a function I will buy one, but don't expect to see me in a cheap suit.

The same person who told me that price was not an Objection also said that anytime anyone contemplates buying anything, there is a mental scale in the brain that goes to work comparing the relative weight of the price and the value. If the price is more important than the value, they will not buy. If the value is more important than the price, they will buy. That is what I want to discover when I ask what they dislike about the product, *the problem they have with the value.*

Ordinarily price is not the Objection. Cost versus value may be. Not the value of the product, but the value as perceived by the prospect. Not the cost of the product, but the cost as perceived by the prospect. Salespeople control the perception the prospect has of the cost of the product, a well as the perception of value.

In one of my classes a lumber salesman questioned the value of sales training. He said, "I can sell a carload of lumber to a prospect, or he can buy the same exact carload of the same lumber for the same price from somebody else and have it delivered the same as I can." It seems to me that the only advantage he would have over the competition would be in the value and in the price as perceived by the client (better selling skills).

Lynne VanDeventer of Prudential Hubbell Real Estate in Lansing, Michigan, sells $15 million worth of homes per year. John sells $1 million worth. They sell the same product, for the same company, in the same area. *They are the same houses at the same price.* Lynne does a better job of giving a higher perception of value, with a lower perception of price. Yes, she does other things better than John, but she talks about the value rather than trying to cut the price.

True, there are times when people cannot afford a particular product, and there are times when people are going to buy on price alone. Sometimes price is a genuine Objection. Sometimes the money is not in the budget, and sometimes there are other constraints that prohibit buying at a particular price. This is where negotiation enters the selling process.

Just as often, prospects use price as a smoke screen because they have some other hidden agenda. Perhaps they don't want to make a decision, or they may be just trying to get rid of us. These could be Put-Offs or possibly Hidden Objections. We should know what the real Objection is, because that is what we have to handle.

No matter how great a job we do handling the wrong Objection, it won't work.

Hidden Objections

I forget the man's name, but I was talking to him about joining a class. His Objection was that he could not take the class on the night of the week it was being offered. He had another commitment. I did not feel this was the true Objection so I said, "I understand how important it is to honor commitments. Other than the fact that you have a problem with that particular night of the week, is there anything else that might be holding you back from joining?" He said, "No." I then said, "So if we were to hold the class on another night, you would be able to make it?" He said, "No." I followed that by saying, "Then, there must be another reason. What might that be?" After a pause, he stated that he would have to check with his wife.

The real problem surfaced only after I used the big *if. If* we could solve this problem, would you go ahead. Then he knew he had to give the real Objection. Of course, having to check with his wife may have been another smoke screen. I kept going and asked what he thought his wife might say. I remember the answer very clearly, "She would probably wonder where I got the guts."

Then I knew the real Objection. He lacked the confidence to get into the class because he had heard about some of the classroom participation he would have to endure. Once I knew that, I went into the Conviction Step and convinced him that he could do it. He joined the class and gained several benefits, one of which was more self-confidence. To answer the original Objection on which night the class was held would have been meaningless.

If we get what we feel is a Hidden Objection, we cushion it by saying, "I understand how you feel." Then we ask, "If we solve this problem, would you go ahead with the purchase?" If they say "Yes," that indicates it was the real Objection, and we can go ahead and handle it by solving the problem, if that is possible. If they say "No," we say, "Then there must be something else holding you back. What might that be?" They tell us, and we go through the same questioning again to find out if they will go ahead if we solve that problem. We continue until the real Objection surfaces. Then we respond to that Objection.

A Put-Off

His name was Bill Kingma. I was talking to him about taking a sales class I knew he did not want to take. He said he really would like to take the class, but could not at this time because he did not have the money.

I treated it just like a Hidden Objection and decided to smoke out the real reason. I asked if there were anything else that was a problem at this time. He said there was not. I asked, "Then what you are saying is, if you had the money, you could join this class?" He said, "Oh yes!" I told him that I had already checked with his boss, and the company would pay for the class. I gave him an enrollment card and asked him to complete it, which he did.

I was not lucky. I had already talked to the boss, who told me that Bill had put off other salespeople. I completed the financial arrangements before I talked to Bill. I also did not tell him what night the course would be offered, so he could not object to that. He just did not want to take the class, but he joined rather than admit that he was not being truthful with me. By the way, Bill did well in the class and went on to become an instructor.

It is not as easy to overcome a Put-Off as it is a Hidden Objection. Often, the prospect is just not sold on our product, and there is no objection to handle. We can handle it like a Hidden Objection, but at the end we just discover that we are being put off. By knowing this, we may prevent wasting our time with them six months from now.

An early Put-Off

Occasionally right at the beginning of a presentation, a prospect will try to get rid of us by a Put-Off. The prospect may not even know what we are selling, and we may not know if it would benefit the prospect. It does not matter. The only purpose of a Put-Off this early in the presentation is to get rid of a salesperson.

For instance, I made my initial contact with a professional who had no disability insurance. He immediately said, "I do not have money for disability insurance after paying all my other insurance premiums." I simply said, "I understand how you feel," and continued with my General Interest Statement. I was successful in setting an appointment to talk about it, because I knew he could not have a genuine objection that early in the presentation.

If prospects give us an Objection even before we have made a presentation, they are probably objecting to our presence. No matter what the Objection, it makes no sense to answer it as a real Objection. It is simply that they do not want to be talking to a salesperson. If we have a possible solution to a problem they have, it is our job to help them see how they may solve that problem. The best way we can do that is to say, "I understand how you feel," and continue with the presentation.

Dennis Deatrick, of Mid-Michigan Bio-Medical, was attending a sales class. The week after we discussed handling Objections, he met with a lab manager about a centrifuge with a bent lid. When he told the price for a new lid, back came the reply, "That is too much money." Dennis said, "I understand how you feel. It is a lot of money," and continued with the presentation.

Dennis told the class that he made the sale because he helped the manager solve her own problem. He also stated that without learning in class how to handle a Put-Off, he would not have known what to do and probably would not have completed the sale.

How Do You Feel about Objections?

Some people say they hate Objections; others say they love to get Objections. I believe they are both nuts. I accept them for what they are, Objections.

Sometimes Objections are valuable because they tell us why we are missing a sale. The same Objection that tends to close the door to a sale also indicates where we can find the key to open the door to the sale. If the prospect says, "I could never learn to operate that," all we have to do is show how easy it is to operate. If the prospect says, "My husband would never go for that," what she is really saying is, "Sell my husband on it."

If you ever want to get rid of pesky salespeople, do not give any Objections because they will just answer them. If you don't give them Objections, they have nothing to answer. Just say, "No thank you," without a reason, no matter what they say. After a couple of "No thank yous," they will leave. The point of this story is that as long as there are Objections, we can keep selling. So don't love Objections, but don't hate them either.

Handling Objections is not a game. It is not like two attorneys dueling in court, each trying to win, not caring if justice is served. We should understand the position of the other party, and look for a way to leave both of us better off than we were before we met. If we lose the sale, it should not be because we gave up on handling the Objections of a prospect who should have bought.

Remember, we will win more often if we answer Objections simply, honestly, and in a manner that shows good taste and understanding for the prospect. That way we can walk arm in arm toward the common objective—*a sale that is beneficial to both of us.*

CHAPTER 13

THE WEIGHING CLOSE

W hat is a nice Close like you doing in a place like this, between the chapters on Handling Objections and the Conviction Step? How come you aren't with the rest of the Closes in Chapter 17? "Even though my name is *Weighing Close*, I am not a *Close*. I am a *Trial Close*." Then why aren't you with the *Trial Closes* in Chapter 16?

"The reason is because I am such a valuable tool right after a Put-Off. A particular type of Put-Off that was not discussed in the last chapter."

Some Background: It seems that nowhere in our K through 12 educational system is there any training in making decisions. Some unsuspecting young couple decides to buy a home. They know about homes because they grew up in one. What they never were confronted with before is a salesperson saying, "This home is yours for only $1,000 per month for the next thirty years. How does that sound?"

Now think about that! $1,000 times twelve months is $12,000 per year, times 30 years is $360,000. "Take a couple of minutes and let me know what your decision is." This example may seem outlandish, but it is what we ask prospects to do occasionally, quickly make a decision to spend large amounts of money, often money they do not even have yet.

What do they do? They say, "We would like to think about it." A Put-Off! What do we do about it? First we say, "I understand how you feel. This is a pretty important decision for you. In all fairness to you and your family, let's take a look at the ideas that might cause you to hesitate, and weigh them against the important reasons to go ahead with this program, and do it right now."

We not only *say*, "I understand how you feel," we *must understand* how they feel. Many times our prospects are faced with the decision of spending large amounts of money that they could be using for something else. They do have an important decision to make, and most of them never had any training in making decisions. The Weighing Close is the best decision-making process I have encountered, either for making a decision of my own or for helping others make a decision. In all fairness, we should share our decision-making training with our prospects.

The Words

- We say, *"Let's* take a look," because we are doing this together with the prospect.

- They are called ideas, not Objections. We do not want to give them the weight of Objections.

- That might cause them to *hesitate*. They will probably buy eventually. They are just hesitating.

- The reasons to go ahead are important.

- We draw a T, and put the minus sign on the left and the plus sign on the right. First we want to list the ideas that might cause them to hesitate. We put down *every* minus that we know they have. Just because we do not write it down here does not mean they will forget about it. We ask them if there is anything else that would cause them to hesitate, until they have no more objections. We do not want any minuses left rattling around.

- Now, let's take a look at the important reasons to go ahead with this _____, and do it right now:

  — List what they said they liked most. List the reasons they said they liked it.
  — List their Primary Interest (what they wanted most in our product).
  — List their Specific Benefits (the reasons they wanted the Primary Interest).
  — List their Dominant Buying Motive (the emotion behind why they wanted the Primary Interest).

- We ask which side weighs more. Either way they decide, we probably have helped them make the right decision.

Again, the Weighing Close is not a Close; it is a Trial Close.

Remember, a Trial Close is not intended to get a decision from the prospect but to get an opinion. We simply want to know where the prospect's mind is at a point in time during the sale. We want to know if the prospect is ready to make a decision. The Weighing Close is an effective method of determining this, even when the prospect is not quite sure what decision to make, or if it is time to do so.

When the prospect says, "The reasons to go ahead weigh more," we still have yet to Close.

CHAPTER 14
THE CONVICTION STEP

T he Conviction Step consists primarily of giving Facts about products and how those Facts will benefit buyers.

When I first started selling mutual funds in California, I was trained in order to get a license. Then I was told to go out and tell people the Facts about mutual funds so they would buy them. Later on, when I  was selling radio time, I talked to prospects about buying space on the air. I told the Facts about our station. When I started selling banquet catering, I told the Facts of our product, the catering service.

When I took my first professional sales class, one of the first comments the instructor made was to instruct us not to give Facts about the product. He said, "People do not buy our product, they buy the product of our product." They buy the Benefit they will derive from our product. He said, "Find out what Benefits they want before you start selling. Let the customer determine your presentation." He was teaching Customer-Driven Sales years before the phrase was coined.

Bill Swietlik sold for Universal Match Company. He said that even though he sold matches, that is not what his customers bought. They bought the advertising on the match cover and what it would do for their business. They did not want to hear about Universal Match Company; they wanted to know what they could accomplish in their business by buying his product.

Because of this advice, I decided I had better not talk about my catering service until I found out what prospects wanted to accomplish with their banquets. I started using this track presentation:

- Attention: To get the prospects to focus on me and to like me.

- General Interest Statement: To get the prospects to want to hear what I could do for them.

- Info: To find out what my prospects want to accomplish, so I know what to talk about.

- Specific Promise: To get the prospects to listen to me and think, "That is exactly what I want, for the very reason I want it."

- Trial Close: To find out if the prospect is ready to buy what I promised I would do for them. (To confirm that they were thinking, "That is exactly what I want, for the very reason I want it.")

Something very interesting happened. Many times when I gave my Specific Promise and asked my Trial Close, "How does that sound?" they would say, "That is exactly what I want."

I had already made the sale, so I did not need to give any Facts and Benefits. We simply started planning the banquet without a Conviction Step. That's right, no Facts or Benefits of our service. They did not want any.

If they wanted a Conviction Step, they would ask for it. They might ask how we could do what others had not been able to do, how something worked, or information on price, structure, or organization. When they asked for Facts about our catering service that were important to them, that is what they got, only those that were important to them. Why bore people with information they do not care to hear?

Because people buy the Benefits of the product, rather than the Facts, each time they got a Fact, they got a Benefit to let them know how it would help them have a successful banquet. That is what was important to them.

As a result of this type of presentation I still had a chance to talk about my product, but only to the extent my prospects were interested, and only in relationship to what it could do for them. I could give a Fact about my catering service and how it would Benefit them.

Back to the examples of banquet catering

- **Specific Promise**: You let my company serve the dinner, and we will do it quickly. All the people will be able to eat together, and they will know you did a good job.

  Question: What enables you to serve quicker than others?

  Fact & Benefit: We have portable food carts so each server makes only one trip from the kitchen instead of many. This means that your guests will be served quickly so they can all eat together. The guests will see how well you've done. **Trial Close**: How does that sound?
- **Specific Promise**: You use my company to serve dinner, and the food will be served hot. That way people will not complain to you, and you need not feel embarrassed.

  Question: How can you make sure the food is served hot?

  Fact & Benefit: We have portable plate warmers and portable steam tables. Hot food goes on hot plates and they are delivered to the table quickly by portable food carts. That will eliminate any complaints or resulting embarrassment. **Trial Close**: Wouldn't that be nice?

- **Specific Promise**: We will serve when we are supposed to and you will not have to spend time in the kitchen. You can spend it with your guests and enjoy yourself.
  Question: How can you promise me that?

Fact & Benefit: We are professionals who serve up to 3,000 people at one meal. It is an easy job for my crew and me to serve your 250 guests. That way there is no need for you to be in the kitchen. Enjoy yourself with the other guests.
Trial Close: That would be nice, wouldn't it?

- **Specific Promise:** I will make sure we do not run out of silverware, so none of your guests will have to eat with spoons. Then your daughter can be proud of her reception.

Question: How do I know you won't run out of silverware?

Fact & Benefit: We have enough silverware for over 3,000 people to eat at once. When we serve your 250 guests, we will have almost twice as much silver there as we need. So you will never have to worry about people eating with spoons and your daughter can be proud of her reception.
Trial Close: You would like that, wouldn't you?

The Fact answers the question, and the Benefit tells why it is important to them. Again, notice that, when possible, the exact words of the prospects are used in stating the Benefits. This eliminates any incorrect interpretation of what they want for this important event.

Follow up with a Trial Close to make sure they agree.

Purposes of the Conviction Step

One purpose of the Conviction Step is to convince our prospects that we have a *good* product for *them*. Notice the two italicized words. We can say something *good* about our product and what it will do for *them* (a *Fact* followed by a *Benefit*).

Another purpose of the Conviction Step is to convince our prospects that our product is *worth* the *money*. Again, notice the two italicized words. When people consider buying something, they mentally weigh *worth*, or value, versus the *money* it will cost.

WORTH   MONEY

On the radio one day I heard a commercial for a bank. I liked it. The ad was for home loans and went something like this: *We are in business to make your life a little better. We have branches all around town, so it is convenient for you to get to us. We train our employees in courtesy, so you enjoy our friendly service. We specialize in prompt service, so as not to waste your time. We give you the interest rate at approval or your closing, whichever is lower. That means you get the best rate possible.*

The reason I liked this commercial was because each time they gave a Fact about the bank, they gave a Benefit. Not only did they give a Benefit, but every Benefit had *"you"* in it. Most people do not care how many branches a bank has, what their training programs consist of, or how their financial policies work. What potential customers want to know is, "What is in it for me?"

Stated alone, a Fact about our product is relatively worthless. We must tell our prospects how that Fact will benefit them.

Stated alone, a Benefit without a Fact is relatively worthless also. The Fact that we have branches all around town makes it believable that we are convenient to get to. The Fact that we use the interest rate at approval or at closing, whichever is lower, makes the Benefit believable, that you get the best rate possible.

Carol Anschuetz sells national television advertising space. Not only does she put a "you" in every Benefit, but she emphasizes the "you," saying it louder than the other words in the Benefit. This is one of the reasons she is very successful. Get the "**You**" in it.

Talk to the Buyer

Assume we are selling desks to a school. In talking to a teacher, here is what we might give as Facts and Benefits. **Fact:** These desks have a smooth, hard top which means, **Benefit:** your students will have better-looking papers, which are easier for you to read.

If talking to maintenance, here is what we could say. **Fact:** These desks have a smooth, hard top which means, **Benefit:** they require less maintenance and are easier for you to clean.

Talking to the school board member who must find the money to pay for the desks, we might say this. **Fact:** These desks have a smooth hard top which means, **Benefit:** they will last longer, remain in service longer, and save you money.

If talking to the purchasing agent, we could say this. **Fact:** These desks have a smooth, hard top which means, **Benefit:** the students will love you because they will have better looking papers, the teachers will love you because the papers will be easier to read, the maintenance people will love you because the desks will be easier to clean, and the school board will love you because it will save money.

All these Facts and Benefits may sound nice, but they may be worthless. All students do not want better looking papers; all teachers do not want papers that are easier to read; all maintenance personnel do not want to make their work easier; all school board members do not want to save money; and all purchasing agents do not want to be loved.

Assume that in the Info we discovered that the purchasing agent wanted a desk with a smooth, hard top because one of the instructors had a problem with scratches on the desks. This instructor was constantly on the PA's case because of those scratches. We certainly should tell the PA, "These desks have a smooth, hard top, resistant to scratches, so you can keep that instructor off your case. How does that sound to you?"

If the purchasing agent asks a question, i.e., "What are these desks made of?" we should answer the question, tie a benefit to it, and Trial Close again. "They are covered with an ultra tough epoxy, which means they will not get any scratches, and that is what would keep the instructor off your case. That would be nice, wouldn't it?"

No More, No Less

Before sending the manuscript of this book to a potential publisher, I requested guidelines to see what they wanted included in a proposal. The publisher asked that the proposal include answers to the following questions:

- Why am I writing the book? How will it serve the reader? Why does the reader need this information? What experiences led me to the knowledge that it imparts?

- What is the competition? If there is none, why not?

- What is the advantage over the competition? What needs will this book fulfill that others do not?

They also wanted a table of contents, suggested reviewers, two sample chapters, and a resume.

What do you think I sent with my proposal? Do you believe that there was anything they wanted that I did not send? Do you think that there were any questions they wanted the answer to that I decided not to answer?

I went down their list and checked it twice to make sure I answered every question they wanted answered. I sent them the table of contents, suggested reviewers, two sample chapters, and a resume. I gave the publisher exactly what was requested. No more, no less.

In a sale it is the same. We give prospects all of the information that they ask for. We give the Facts that they have requested, and follow them with the Benefits that they said were important to them. No more, no less.

Yes, we must make sure we give a Benefit after every Fact, so our prospects will know what that particular Fact will do for them. They buy the Benefits of our product, but only those that they are interested in. Make sure the Benefit applies to that particular prospect, not everyone else in the same job.

A prospect's motivation to buy is personal. Benefits must be based on the information he or she gives us in the Info. If we did not find out what Benefits he or she wanted during the Info, we should have. It enables us to talk in terms of the customer's interest. That is all he or she is interested in.

Judy Fowler is an R.N. and Salesperson for Diversified Medical Group. They sell services to nursing homes in the Midwest. Judy said that the majority of the administrators to whom she sells make the decision to use Diversified without ever knowing what company she represents. All they know and care about is that they have some problems that Judy has convinced them she can solve.

When to Use a Conviction Step

Here are the rules on when to use a Conviction Step:

1. When the prospect asks for it, by asking questions.
2. When the prospect has not asked for it, but we feel it is necessary.

That is right. Give only those Facts and Benefits in which your prospect is interested. If you do not feel your prospect is interested in any, do not give any. If prospects have questions, they will ask. When you get a question, answer it, tie a Benefit to it, and Trial Close.

The second purpose of the Conviction Step is to convince prospects our product is worth the money. Cost is measured in relationship to what they get in return. They have a mental scale that automatically weighs value against cost. We can try to reduce the cost or we can try to increase the value on the prospect's mental scale. If the product is really worth the price, we should emphasize the product's value, the value to the prospect.

Review

If we do not Close right after the Specific Promise but go into the Conviction Step, we give only those Facts about our product in which the prospect is interested, followed by their related Benefits. Then we Trial Close.

If we only give those Facts and Benefits in which the prospect is interested, we put the prospect in position to agree with everything we say. The prospect will never say, "But that is not important to me."

Still another purpose of the Conviction Step is to get people to believe that what we say about our product is true. After all, prospects do not believe everything salespeople say. How to address that problem is discussed in the next chapter.

CHAPTER 15

GETTING PROSPECTS TO BELIEVE WHAT WE SAY

The third purpose of the Conviction Step is to get prospects to believe what we say is true. Obviously, not everyone believes all the things salespeople say. We do not want to have to prove everything we say, so we go back to the same rule that applies when we give a Conviction Step. We give evidence when our prospects ask for it, or when they do not ask but we believe it is necessary.

Most of what I have heard or read about getting people to believe what we say is true is associated with evidence. There are other methods to accomplish the same thing. These methods help us reduce the amount of evidence we have to give, and at the same time make what we say more believable.

Tell the Truth: If we limit ourselves to the truth, a certain segment of the population will believe more of what we say. If we get caught in a lie or an exaggeration, much or all of what we say from then on is suspect. Do what your mom taught you! Tell the truth!

Understate: When I applied for a contract with Northwestern Mutual, the general agent asked what my grade point was at Michigan State University. I told him it was above a 3.2. That was one of the first things he checked, and found it was a 3.4. Later, he told me that because of the understatement, he did not have to check on some other statements I had made.

An advertisement by Northwestern Mutual Life stated that the company ranked first in a study of low cost more often than any other company over the last eighteen years. The ad quoted Best's, a firm which rates life insurance companies. That is understatement. The actual figures showed that Northwestern ranked first in seventeen of those eighteen years. People will believe the good things we say about ourselves if we practice humility.

First Tell What It Will Not Do, Then What It Will Do: In 1955, I bought an Austin Healey 100 sports car. The ad said something like, "It may not do 120, but we guarantee it will do 110." It must have been an impressive ad. I have remembered it for thirty-seven years. I believed it would do 120 mph. It did.

When selling a retirement annuity with a guarantee of $100,000 upon retirement, one could say, "This guarantee by itself will not give you a great retirement, but the $100,000 will help to make retirement a little brighter."

When selling a small room air conditioner, one could say, "This room air conditioner will not cool the entire house on a hot day, but it will surely help you get a good sleep on the hot summer nights."

Work on a Referral Basis: Get prospects by referral. We can ask clients to give us referrals to friends, relatives, and business associates. Along with the referral comes a certain amount of trust. People tend to believe us more if we are sent to them by someone they respect. That is one of the primary reasons that referrals are the best prospects.

Sell Yourself: Dale Carnegie's book, *How to Win Friends and Influence People*, has nine basic rules for selling yourself. Read the book or, better yet, take a Dale Carnegie Course. If we use these rules, people will like us better. If they like us better, they will believe more of what we say.

Evidence

Evidence as an Attention Step: Sometimes we may use Evidence in the Attention Step. This can eliminate the possibility of it being requested later on when we do not want it to interrupt our presentation.

While waiting for my prospect in a CPA firm, I found a copy of *Fortune* magazine. In it was a survey on the most respected companies as rated by their peers. My company was rated number one in the industry. I used his copy of *Fortune* as my Attention Step and did not have to worry about giving Evidence about the quality of my company.

If I were selling automobiles and I found a newspaper article that stated one of my products was rated at 54 miles per gallon, I could use that as an Attention Step. Then I would not have to use Evidence to back up a statement on the good gas mileage later on. One advantage of using the Evidence ahead of time is that it keeps doubt from creeping into the mind of the prospect.

When Do We Give Evidence? We give Evidence when the prospects ask for it. We also give Evidence when they do not ask for it, but we feel it is required anyway. If an independent survey has rated our company number one in some important area, such as quality or price, we should use that Evidence, even if they do not ask for it. We cannot expect our prospects to believe we are number one just because we say so. Every other salesperson in the same business can make the claim that they are number one. In this case we should give Evidence to prove that we are telling the truth.

What Is the Difference between Proof and Evidence? Evidence is a statement, an exhibit, or demonstration that tends to prove what we say is true. It is said that Proof is personal. The same Evidence given to different people will be Proof to some but not to others. As in a jury trial, where the same Evidence is given to all jurors, some will accept it as Proof and some will need more Evidence.

Therefore, if we wish to prove that something we say about our product is true, we must be concerned whether that Evidence is accepted by our prospects as Proof. We can do this by tailoring our Evidence to the client. If we are working with accountants, statistics might be the best form of Evidence. Others might be confused or bored by statistics. A graph may work better for an engineer, or a trade magazine for someone who works in the same field as we do.

The simpler the better. When I was brand new in the life insurance business my manager was trying to prove to me how good the company's product was by explaining a ledger to me. He explained it for about twenty minutes, and I still had no idea what he was talking about. He made a couple of mistakes. First, it was too complicated. He knew the jargon of insurance. I did not. Second, I was not interested in it, so he should not have showed it to me in the first place.

Forms of Evidence

Demonstrations: Demonstrations can be fun when used like a game or a play. They are interesting to watch, which means they are usually effective. They are even better if we can get the prospect involved. (You hold onto this end and I will grab the other to see if we can pull them apart.) Make sure the prospect does not look bad in the demonstration. It should be an enjoyable experience.

Practice the demonstration ahead of time to make sure it works. I watched a salesman stand on an aluminum pop can to prove it would not squash under his 200-pound weight. He crushed it, proving just the opposite of what he intended to prove. When the salesman first saw the demonstration, it had been done with a pop can which had a seam: the seam kept it from being squashed. The salesman made the mistake of using a seamless can. No, he made the mistake of not practicing the demonstration first. Make sure your demonstration works before you try it in front of prospects.

When a window salesman told me that he always gives a demonstration, I asked him if he would hold off letting someone buy in order to give a demonstration. He said, "No." I told him, "You may be doing just that every time you give a demonstration that is not required."

Exhibits: I have seen cutaways of tires, windows, insulation, dishwashers, fireplaces, golf balls, just about anything imaginable. They all serve the purpose of proving something to somebody. We just have to make sure that what we are proving is relevant to the prospect. I do not want to see how well a window is insulated when my problem is that I cannot get the dumb things apart to get them cleaned.

The exhibit does not have to be a model or a cutaway. Many times it is the actual product, such as a household appliance or

business machine. An exhibit can be just about anything that can be picked up or that takes up space. It can be the entire product or just part of the product. It can be a picture, a video, or a graph. The more interesting it is, the more memorable and the better it is.

A speaker talking to salespeople selling windows, doors, and siding said, "Every time you sell windows, show a cutaway of how they are made so you make your presentation more interesting." Beware of this advice. Exhibits are only interesting to those who are interested in that particular evidence; to the rest, it is boring. Not only that, but if you show prospects things they are not interested in, they will know you are not interested in them.

Testimonials: We can have a written testimonial about every major benefit of our product. We simply go around to see our satisfied clients and determine what impressed them about our product. After they tell us what impressed them most, we ask if we could get it in writing. Most of them will say, "Yes." We get a testimonial on all the major aspects of our product: reliability, ease of operation, what their employees or families liked about it, how it solved a particular problem, cost of operation.

One problem we will encounter is that even though clients are quick to agree to give a testimonial, many times the testimonials are not forthcoming. We really cannot press them for it or they will become unhappy clients. What we can do is tell them that we can save them time by writing the letter for them. We ask for a letterhead, have it written to their approval, and we have them sign it.

Later on, when a different prospect questions how difficult it will be for the employees to learn how to use our product, we pull out the letter from XYZ Company. It tells how happy the employees of XYZ were that the product was easy to learn to use. This letter may be several paragraphs long, so to conserve the prospect's time, highlight the portion that states that the product was easy to learn to use. That makes the process simpler and more relevant for the prospect.

If we do not have a written testimonial for evidence on a particular aspect of our product, we can give a verbal testimonial. For example, I might use the following: "Bob Crosby of Community News said, 'The major benefit I received from the sales class was the confidence I gained from using a track. It allows me to talk to any prospect, and remain in control of the presentation.'"

Examples: An example is similar to a verbal testimonial in that it is a story about the benefit someone received from our product. The key difference is that an example is a story *about* someone, rather than *by* that person. In the verbal testimonial of Bob Crosby, in the previous paragraph, the testimonial is what he said. If I just told what Bob did, it would be an example.

A word of caution on testimonials or examples used as Evidence. We should not use the testimonial or example of a competitor of the prospect. Many times our prospects have no respect for their competitors. Once, a salesperson for a restaurant called me. They had a coupon book, with which I could buy one meal and get another free. They gave me the name of another insurance agent who had taken advantage of the offer. I had been considering the offer, until the salesperson mentioned the name of the other agent.

Statistics: Statistics bore many people. If the prospect is interested in statistics, we use them; if the prospect is not interested, they are not of much value. I seldom use statistics published by my own company. So many times I have heard, "Any company can use statistics to prove they are the best." Consider using statistics published by an unbiased third-party to sound more believable.

In my briefcase I carry many third-party statistics. I have evidence for just about every aspect of my company, ready to use when they prove what I want to prove, and when the prospect is interested. I am very careful to make sure I only use those statistics that are important to my prospects. I want excited prospects, not bored ones.

Analogies: I like using analogies, two dissimilar ideas with something in common. We compare what prospects may not understand to something they do understand.

Consider, for example, the following analogies:

- Diversifying your investments is like not putting all your eggs in one basket. One mistake will not wipe you out.

- Money left in your checkbook will disappear like an ice cube held in your hand. Put it where it will not melt away.

- Life insurance is property, just like your house. Unless you sign it over, nobody else has any rights to change it without your permission.

- Evidence is like a crutch. It is great to have it when you need it, but just like a crutch, if you use it when you don't need it, you are going to impede your progress.

Facts

One of the best types of Evidence and one that is constantly overlooked is a Fact. Just as with any other form of evidence, we give Facts only when prospects have asked for them or if we feel they are needed. We have all learned that a Fact without a Benefit to the prospect is usually worthless. A Benefit without a Fact is no better.

If I say, "You will get great service," that is a Benefit, but it is also a claim that people may not believe is true. If we put a Fact in front of that Benefit it changes the statement to one that is more believable. "We have an 800 number that connects to a staff of ten service reps twenty-four hours per day which means that you will get great service."

Sometimes rather than stating a Fact followed by a Benefit, salespeople state a Benefit followed by a Benefit, which is still unbelievable. All they have done is to state a claim followed by a claim. "We have a good bunch of service technicians which means that you will get great service." The statement that we have a good bunch of service technicians adds no credibility to the Benefit. To make the Benefit "you will get great service" believable, it must be preceded by a Fact.

So what is a Fact in selling? Ordinarily a Fact is simply a true statement, but not so in selling. In selling a Fact is considered to be something that people will accept as being true. A claim is something that people will not accept as being true. A sale takes place in the prospect's mind, therefore what the prospect believes or does not believe is what is important. If a prospect believes what we say, we do not have to give Evidence. If a prospect does not believe what we say, we must give Evidence even though what we said is true. That is the purpose of Evidence, to get prospects to believe what we say is true.

Generally specific is better

One way to get people to believe what we say is to be very specific in our facts. Back to the examples of banquet catering. Assume that a party of 100 people had a problem with cold food in the past. We could say, "We have some great food warming equipment and that will make sure your party gets hot food." They may not believe that is enough Evidence. If we get specific and say, "We will use electric plate and food warmers for your party and that will make sure your party gets hot food," it becomes more believable.

We could make it even more specific and therefore even more believable. "I will reserve a portable steam table and two plate warmers that will each hold fifty plates for your party. That will make sure that hot food is put onto hot plates. Then we can serve it immediately to your guests to make sure your party gets hot food."

The more specific we are, the more believable we are. The Benefit is the same in each of these three statements; only the Fact is more specific. Be specific in your Facts and people will believe more in your Benefits.

It is better not to be specific or exact all of the time. An engineer or accountant would generally require more specificity than an salesperson. An engineer estimated the cost of installing sewers in our subdivision. His estimate in typical engineer fashion: $5,865,343.05. I believe he rounded it off to the nearest nickel.

Remember! Tailor the Evidence to the prospect.

Remember! We give Evidence either when the Prospect asks for it or when we feel it is necessary, even if it's not requested.

Remember! A great time to Trial Close is immediately after giving Evidence.

CHAPTER 16

BUYING SIGNALS AND TRIAL CLOSES

W
hen I was studying leadership in the Army in Fort Riley, Kansas, the question was asked: "Assume you have come to a river that has stopped your advance. The river is seventy-five feet across, and you have only fifty feet of bridge to use in crossing it. What is the order you give to get the bridge across the river in order to get your troops to the other side?"

The answer is, *"Sergeant, put that bridge across that river."* This sounds so simplistic, but it is the proper answer. It is the only answer.

I mention this story as there is a question in sales that has an answer just as simplistic. "When is the right time to ask for the order?" The proper answer is, *"When the prospect is ready to buy."* That is also the only answer. The purpose of this chapter is to teach you how to determine when the prospect is ready to buy.

During a presentation, our prospects get closer and closer to the point when they are ready to buy. If we continue talking and selling, we start talking them out of it. In effect, we sell the product, and then buy it back. *The sale takes place in the mind of the prospect*, and we must know where that mind is at all times, especially when we are getting near the point when we should ask for the order. That is the time to successfully close the sale.

Buying Signals

A Buying Signal, sometimes called a Closing Clue, Closing Signal, or Interest Indicator, is anything our prospects say or do that could indicate they are ready to buy. Notice the weasel word "could." Just because we get a Buying Signal does not mean our prospects are definitely going to buy. It generally is a signal of interest. Whether or not they are ready to buy depends on the level of interest. We must be able to read the signals correctly. If the Buying Signal is ignored, it may cost us the sale because it rarely happens that someone will say directly, "I am ready to buy."

Some signals are easy to read. Let's say you are talking to your teenage son and you say, "Son, you know what I ought to do? I ought to let you use my new Mercedes 340SL for your date tonight, instead of your old clunker." Can you see his head bobbing up and down, agreeing with you? Can you hear him say, "Yeah! Yeah!" Can you see his eyes get larger and larger? He might lean closer, to make sure he heard right. He may even offer to get you a cup of coffee or a Coke. At least he will get friendlier. I can hear him asking where the keys are, see him becoming somewhat antsy to get moving.

These are common Buying Signals. Prospects who are interested nod their heads, agree with us, and sometimes say "Yeah!" They will get antsy to do something. Their eyes get larger, they lean toward us, they act friendlier, and they ask questions that indicate they may be ready to buy.

Chapter 16   Buying Signals and Trial Closes

If we continue to sell right through all these signals, the prospect's enthusiasm may die. This means we just bought back the product without commission. This chapter might be exciting for you to read, but if it drags on, and on, and on, you will give up on it. In sales, prospects give up if we go on, and on, and on.

The normal **nonverbal** Buying Signals are easy to list: getting friendlier; nodding the head; offering a cup of coffee or a soft drink; certain movements, such as leaning closer or sitting back and relaxing. Almost anything out of the ordinary could be an indicator.

Grady McKay, former National Sales Trainer for The Dale Carnegie Sales Course, would watch his prospects' eyes. He said that when people accept what we say, their pupils become enlarged. He said that signal is involuntary, they cannot hide it.

During a sales class I mentioned that while giving a talk, speakers can pick up Buying Signals that indicate if members of the audience agree with their talk. Many times the speaker will subconsciously seek out the interested ones. I told the class that if we nod our heads during the talk, we can capture the eye contact of the speaker.

Later on during the class, one of the students, Jennifer Simmons, was making a presentation in front of the class. As she talked, I could see that, for the majority of the time, she was looking at someone in back of the room. I looked in the back and there was another student, Lori Paternoster, nodding her head in agreement.

Later, I asked Jennifer where she was looking during her talk. She said she was looking all around, and at nobody in particular. I asked the class, and they said she was looking at someone in back of the room. I asked Lori, who said, "She was looking at me, because I was nodding my head."

The point of this story is that Jennifer did not realize she was reacting to Lori. Often prospects do not realize they are giving us Buying Signals. *We must realize that they are indicating they may be ready to buy now.*

Verbal Buying Signals

Verbal buying signals are different. Sometimes they are in the form of questions which are relatively easy to recognize. Sometimes they are in the form of objections. Then we have to determine if it really is a Buying Signal, or a smoke screen which would let us know they are not interested. Sometimes Buying Signals are in the form of conversation between two people we are talking to. It may be a Buying Signal when one asks the other a question.

"Does it come in white?"

Questions: Someone may ask, "How large is your company?" Why would anyone care how large my company is, unless there was an interest? "Can this be paid on a monthly basis?" Why the interest in how to pay for it, unless there is an interest in buying it? People are not concerned about how to pay for something unless they are thinking about buying it. Asking how to pay for something is a pretty strong Buying Signal. The same is true of questions about options, delivery details, or choices of color, design, or size.

Key Words: Sometimes as we go through the Info prospects may use some key words that indicate an interest in what we are selling. These are words like *necessary*, *need*, *have to*, words that indicate they have no real choice.

For instance, when talking about investment programs, a prospect may state something about needing to have one or how it may be necessary. When people talk about something being necessary, they are in effect saying, "I have no choice. This is something I have to do." Occasionally people will make reference to it being a necessary evil.

Chapter 16   Buying Signals and Trial Closes

They may be saying that they do not like the product, but they are also saying that they must have it anyway.

Sometimes when I'm talking with a manager about a class in Customer-Driven Sales, somewhere in the initial contact, the person might say something like, "Yeah, this is what all sales is coming to lately." Not an enthusiastic response, but clearly a Buying Signal; the manager is saying he may not like it, but he needs it. So, listen to the words that prospects use. Sometimes they give an indication of the possibility of making a sale.

Objections: Sometimes prospects will not ask about different ways of paying for the product. Instead, they make an Objection: "We just cannot come up with that much for a down payment."

Why would they be concerned about not being able to come up with a down payment, unless they were interested in the product? They may be asking if we could lower the down payment, or they may be asking for help in finding the money. They may be indicating that they probably should see something for less money. Either way, this Objection is a pretty strong Buying Signal.

When we get an Objection we should ask ourselves, "Why did they ask that? Is it a buying signal?" We can find out by using a Trial Close. A Trial Close is never out of place.

If we are talking to a couple, or to two or more people, we should also listen to the conversation between them. Many times, one will ask the other a question as if we were not present. A wife may ask her husband, "What do you think of it?" This may indicate she is interested, or it may be that she is not interested and hopes he is not. Either way, she has just done us a favor by Trial Closing him. We should really be interested in the answer.

What do we do when we get a Buying Signal? If it is very strong, and we feel it is time to Close, then we should Close. If it's not so strong, and we want to find out if it is time to close, then we should Trial Close. We do not want to ask for the order unless we know we are going to get it, or at least have a good feeling we will get a positive response. A negative response to a Close sets us back further than we were before we asked.

Trial Closes

We discussed Trial Closes in Chapter 9, using one after the Specific Promise. A Trial Close is a question we ask anytime during the sales presentation to determine how near the prospect is to closing, to find out if it is time to ask for the order. The purpose, we must remember, is to get an *opinion*, not a decision. The *decision* comes in the Close.

Grady McKay left his sales territory in western Michigan to become Director of Sales Training for The Dale Carnegie Sales Course. He was in charge of training the salespeople who sold the course. I took over his old territory and because of this, I had the opportunity to spend much time with him and gain valuable training.

I was riding with Grady one day, discussing my method of selling the Dale Carnegie Sales Course. He asked me if I used Trial Closes. I said that I did. He asked me to give him a Trial Close. I did. Grady said, "That is not a Trial Close, that is a Close." He asked for another with the same result. "That is not a Trial Close, that is a Close." I did not know the difference. I do now.

I teach a class in sales at Lansing Community College, and we use a text that was written by some college professors who do not know the difference. In one place the text says that a Trial Close is, "A closing attempt made at opportune times during the sales presentation." If Grady McKay were here, he would say, "That is not a Trial Close, that is a Close."

A closing attempt is a Close. In a Trial Close we are not trying to close; we are only soliciting an opinion. We are trying to determine if the prospect is ready to buy. In the Close we try to get the prospect to take action. After a successful Trial Close, we know if the prospect would like to own the product. After a successful Close, the customer owns the product.

A Trial Close is similar to a Buying Signal except that we initiate the Trial Close, while the prospect initiates the Buying Signal. A prospect can say with actions or words, "I like the product" (Buying Signal). I can ask my prospect, "Do you like the product?" (Trial Close). I did not ask for the order but only asked what the prospect thinks about the product. Buying Signals and Trial Closes serve the same purpose.

> A **Close** asks for a decision: "Will this be cash or charge?"
>
> A **Trial Close** asks for an opinion: "Do you prefer using cash or a charge card?"
>
> (Most Trial Closes are not modified Closes, although they can be as in the cash or charge example above.)

In selling real estate, here are some possible Trial Closes.

- What do you think of the size of the bedrooms?

- Do you think your furniture will fit in here?

- How do you feel about $10,000 for a down payment?

- Do you feel you can fit $650 per month into your budget?

- If you decide to buy this home, will you want the drapes included?

- What do you think your husband will say, if you tell him you want to buy this home?

- How do you like it?

- What do you think of it?

Notice that the words "think" and "feel" show up quite often in Trial Closes. That is because we are trying to find out what prospects think or feel about what we are selling. What they think or feel is what is in their heads that we cannot hear. All we have to do is ask the proper way and they will tell us what they are thinking or feeling. That way we can determine when they are ready to buy.

The Trial Closes listed above can be used in almost any type of sale, including working with purchasing agents. In the sale of real estate as well as with other products, the person making the decision usually acts as a agent, buying for himself or herself and for other users. Does that make sense? (That is a Trial Close.) Look again at the sample real estate Trial Closes and see how they fit what you sell.

If, in answer to a Trial Close, my prospects reply that they have not yet made a decision, I let them know I understand that. I then tell them that I just wanted to find out what they thought about the product. Then I Trial Close again.

Progressive Trial Closes

We can develop Progressive Trial Closes for our own products, wherein we ask a series of questions designed to lead naturally to the Close. Similar to Information Gathering Questions, these start with the less threatening questions and move to the more threatening questions just before the actual Close. The purpose is to effect a smooth transition from presentation to Close. These questions are very effective, but only if we know them so well we can rattle them off in our sleep.

When I sell a sales course I tell the prospects the Benefits they will receive from taking the class (Specific Promise); then I ask, "How does that sound?" or, "Is that what you want?" If I have done a good job, they will say, "Yes, it sounds great." Then I ask, "Would that be worth thirty hours of your time?" They say, "Yes." Next, "Would that be worth an investment of $$ (the price)?" If they say "Yes," I ask them to fill in the enrollment form. I can assume they are ready to complete the form and join the class because of their answers to the Trial Closes.

Buying Signals and Trial Closes are indicators. They indicate that prospects are interested to varying degrees, and that prospects *may* or *may not* be ready to buy or *are* ready to buy. The more we practice Trial Closes, the better they work for us and the better our closing ratios.

It sure beats guessing.

CHAPTER 17

THE CLOSE

M ost people who take a class in sales or selling seem to want to learn how to close effectively more than any other aspect of selling. When they finish the class, they usually realize that a good closer is merely a good salesperson and how simple a Close really is.

A few recent books call it the Action Step. I use the word "Close" as that is the terminology commonly used in sales. It is true that action must take place, however, because the purpose of the Close is to get *favorable action*. In Customer-Driven Sales, the results of a successful Close should be favorable to both the buyer and the seller. Both parties should be better off than they were before.

The Successful Close

Notice that the word sale is not mentioned as being the result of a successful Close. In many situations the Close precipitates a sale or a contract, but many times a successful Close is only a step toward the sale or contract.

While selling training to an organization that had over fifteen branches, I did not walk in and make a sale on the first interview, or even within the first month. The goal of the first Close was to get in to see the next level of management. It was successful: The action that was taken enabled me to set up a meeting with the director of training.

With the director of training, I had a successful Close, which resulted in my being introduced to the person who would check out my training capabilities. Although I closed successfully, no money changed hands, there was no contract and no sale. But there certainly was favorable action.

When I met with the person who could make the final recommendation, I made my Presentation. That person was impressed with what benefits could accrue to the branches, and I was impressed with the remuneration I would receive. Again I asked for the order and received favorable action. The favorable action was a recommendation to the director of training that I start training at the branches. Still no money, no sale, and no contract, but I sure judged it to be a successful Close.

I was contacted and asked to submit a written proposal. I submitted the proposal and it was accepted. That was a successful Close resulting in a sale, a contract, and money.

There are other times that I had four, five, and six meetings which eventually led to a sale. There were no Put-Offs involved. In each case there was a Presentation which resulted in the action I wanted. That is the purpose of a Close, to get favorable action.

The more sophisticated the Presentation, the more complicated the Presentation, and the more expensive the product, the more Closes there will be before the sale is consummated. The last of these Closes is the one that people usually refer to as a Close.

The Close Most Salespeople Seek

The best action we can get in the final Close is payment in full, along with a signature. The next best is partial payment, along with a signature. If no money is exchanged, another form of signature is next best, a signature on a note. If we cannot get any of those, a signature will have to do. If we can get nothing else, a handshake is better than nothing.

There has to be some sort of obligation for the buyer because a post-sale letdown occurs in so many sales. The prospect wonders, "Did I do the right thing, or am I just wasting my money?" Some decide against completing the sale, unless they are obligated. People have varying degrees of obligation. For some it is a promise, for others a handshake, and for others, even a signature and payment in full are barely enough.

A Close is a contract. For a contract to be valid, there must be an offer and an acceptance. In many cases, either the offer or the acceptance must include money or it is not a valid contract. For that reason, get the money. If you cannot get the money, get a signature. Do something to cause the buyer to feel obligated to honor the sale.

In most cases, the question is not whether there is a valid contract but is there a sale? When selling insurance, one can complete an application with or without money. Notwithstanding the legal aspects of contracts, there is probably a 20 percent better chance of ending up with a sale and a commission if money is included with the application. If there is no money up front, the sale must be made again when returning for the money.

It's the same sort of situation as working for a building contractor I know. The first job subcontractors have is to convince the building contractor to hire them. The second job is to do the actual work. The most difficult job comes later, trying to get paid for the work they did.

I used to wear a pin with the insignia of the company I worked for. There was an inscription in Latin on it. One day I asked what the inscription was in English. I was told it meant, "Get the money." Later I discovered exactly what that meant. If I did not get the money with the signature, I had less than a 50 percent chance of getting paid for the sale. The buyers never showed up. They were like "be backs" in the retail trade. They say they will "be back," but they never return.

Why do I spend so much verbiage here on getting the money?

Don't get the money and you will discover why.

We Close when the prospects are ready to buy. We discover when they are ready to buy by watching and listening for Buying Signals and by using Trial Closes. If we do this well, we will not have to ask prospects if they want to buy but only how they want to buy. We use an Assumed Close.

The Assumed Close

When I started in sales, my two sons were quite young. Phil would eat anything, while Scott would eat only what he wanted, which was not much. I decided that I did not want to make him eat what he did not want, except during a trial period. I felt it was part of his education to try every food my wife put on the table.

If she served peas, which he did not like, I asked him to take a serving of peas. If he took the serving, fine, but if he did not, I would ask him if he wanted one spoonful or two. He learned to say, "I'll take one, Dad." I was not interested in finding out if he would eat peas, but how many. That was an Assumed Close.

It is the same in selling. I am not interested in giving the prospect a choice of whether to buy or not to buy, but only how to buy. If our prospects indicate that we have a good product for them, they believe it is worth the money, and feel they should have it, we should ask *how* they want to pay for it rather than *if* they want to pay for it. We may ask them if they want it *delivered* rather than if they want to *buy* it.

We should show them where to sign, or to whom to make out a check, or to whom to give the money, or any other instruction that will make it easier for them to buy.

We can offer a choice of two methods of buying; it could be a choice of one of two styles, sizes, colors, or even one of two ways of paying for the purchase.

One way or the other, we should assume our prospects are going to buy. If we do not believe they are going to buy, we should not be closing.

Before I got involved in sales, I hated it when a hard sell salesperson would assume a Close on me when I did not want the product. So, why would I ever advocate an Assumed Close and do it to someone else? When I assume my prospects are going to buy, it is based on information they have given to me. I dislike a salesperson trying to bulldoze me into buying, but I like it when he or she makes it easy for me to buy.

Minor Point Close: We give them one choice. "Do you want this delivered?" "Would you like to pay cash for this?" "Can you take a physical exam today?"

Alternate Close: Two choices. "Do you want this delivered, or would you rather take it with you?" "Will this be cash or charge?" "Can you take a physical exam today, or would you rather I set it up for tomorrow?"

Instructional Close: "Please make the check out to Northwestern." "Please write the address for delivery on this line." "Let's call right now and set up a physical."

Shut Up!

That's right, shut up! After the Close, shut up. When you ask if this will be cash or charge, shut up. If I ask which would be better for a physical, today or tomorrow, I have to shut up while waiting for a response. If we experience an uncomfortable silence, that's OK, but we have to shut up. Let the prospect be uncomfortable; let the prospect think. We take our prospects off the hook when we talk; we mess up their train of thought, and we blow the sale.

Shut Up Again: That's right, shut up one more time. After we get the order, no stories, no jokes, no anecdotes, no selling. Congratulate them to counteract any post-sale letdown they may have, and go away.

A retired Air Force colonel was looking at a house which was located across the street from a clubhouse. He decided to buy it and make his home there. As he and the real estate agent were leaving to sign the papers, the agent said, "Having been in the service, you will appreciate the fact that there is a band concert each Sunday at the clubhouse across the street." That killed the sale.

Get referrals; Yes. Write them a thank-you note; Yes. Let them know you feel they made a wise decision; Yes. Tell a joke; No. Tell another story; No. Keep selling; No. Just go!

Actually there is something you can say and do after the Close that may help you become more professional and possibly richer, but only after an unsuccessful Close: Ask why you did **not** get the order.

While selling glass, Jerry Flowers made a proposal to furnish the windows for a large apartment building. He said that he was sitting in his car feeling sorry for himself because he had missed that big sale. He got to thinking and realized that he did not even know why he lost the sale. He returned to the decision maker and asked why.

The man told him that his price was $1500 too high. Jerry asked, "If I drop my price below the other proposal, can I get the contract?" The man said, "Yes," and Jerry ended up with the largest sale he had ever made.

It is almost the same in any step of the sales process; if there is a question you have, usually the person who has the answer is standing right there in front of you. Ask and you shall receive.

Listen and watch for Buying Signals. Trial Close to see if it is time to Close. When it is time, do not ask if they are going to buy, but only how or how much, some other form of assumption. Then be quiet. If we practice this and do it faithfully, we will be able to close without fear, without fail, and without fumbling. Both we and our prospects will be better off than before we met.

Wouldn't that be a nice feeling?

CHAPTER 18

I LIKE A TWO-STEP SALE

When selling the Dale Carnegie Course, I kept a record of each day's activity. After selling for a while, I would total my number of phone calls, in-person calls, closes, sales, income, etc. Every once in a while I would compare ratios to see where I had become more effective and where I needed to improve.

One set of ratios stood out above all others: my closing ratio when I talked to a new prospect only once versus my closing ratio when I spoke to the prospect twice. When I made a Presentation on the first contact, only 32 percent of my closes were successful. When I made my first contact by phone or on a three-minute cold call, the success ratio was 69 percent. The difference was dramatic enough that I eliminated the one-step sale except where I felt I had a sure sale.

Based on my ratios, I found that with a one-step sale I was not only losing more than half of my potential prospects, but it meant doing twice as much prospecting as required, and more paperwork than I needed. I was not as effective as I could be.

So I became a two-step salesperson. The first step was a cold call to set up a future Presentation or a phone call to set up a future Presentation. The second step included Attention, General Interest, Info, Specific Promise, and Close.

I do not know the reason I had greater success setting an appointment on the first contact and completing the Presentation on the second. I was not too concerned with the reasons why. I just took advantage of the information and became more effective.

An interesting sidelight to this was the revelation that if after the second call I was put off for any reason, my closing ratio went down to about 20 percent when I went back to try closing later. As a result of this information, I eliminated the third call.

Asking for an appointment on the first contact and then making a Presentation on the second is not the typical two-step sale. It is covered here because some salespeople ask about the advantages of a one-step, do-it-all Presentation. The key is for each person to keep records and find out what actually happens in his or her own style of selling.

The Two-Step Sale

In many forms of selling the information can be gathered, but a Presentation during the same interview at the same time would be less than perfect. Many times graphs, documentation, or research requires that another appointment be set in order to make the final Presentation for the prospect's acceptance. In this case, the first steps are the same as in a regular one-step sale:

- **Attention:** We get the prospect to like and focus on us.

- **General Interest:** We tell the prospect generally what we have done for others and feel we can do for him or her.

- **Bridge to Info:** We tell the prospect, "In order to determine how much benefit you can receive, and to conserve your time, may I ask you some questions?"

- **Info:** Fact-Finding and Feeling-Finding Questions. Determine the prospect's Primary Interest, Specific Benefits, and Dominant Buying Motive.

- **Specific Promise:** We promise prospects that we can satisfy their Primary Interest, give them the Specific Benefits they want, and gratify their Dominant Buying Motive. We tell them that in order to accomplish this, we should set another appointment. Set the next appointment at that time.

If we were in real estate, helping someone find a home, we would have to terminate the interview after the first meeting and set up a second appointment. Between the first appointment and the second, we would gather the information required to find a home that matched the prospect's needs. When we met the prospect for the second appointment, we would be prepared to show homes professionally.

Unless time is of the essence, professional real estate agents do not show homes to prospects until they have had the chance to see the homes and gain the product knowledge necessary to make an intelligent presentation.

In attempting to get a listing to sell a home, we would probably not have any reason to do a two-step sale. We would use the track: find the prospect's Primary Interest, Specific Benefits, and Dominant Buying Motive; give the Specific Promise; and Close.

Sometimes, we expect to make a one-step sale, until we gather the information. Then we find that in order to complete our presentation, we need to change to a two-step sale. This happens often in selling insurance or investments. It is always best to set the next appointment before leaving.

If it is a simple single-need sale, it can be done in one sitting. If it is complicated, we need time to prepare a Presentation that is relevant and understandable. There are times when we find that we need evidence that we do not have with us. Sometimes research is required, while other times we simply run out of time. When necessary, we must know how to achieve an organized two-step sale.

There is one major disadvantage to the two-step sale: *memory*. We do not remember all that was said during the Info, *and the prospect does not remember either.* In a one-step sale, immediately after we listen to the answers given in the Info, we can remember the exact words given by the prospect. We can promise in the Specific Promise exactly what the prospect wants, and do so in the prospect's words. Days later, when neither of us remembers the exact words, our promise to solve the prospect's problem becomes less effective, or often ineffective.

This means that either during the Info, or immediately after, we must write down exactly what our prospects say.

The Second Step

Second Step Format

1. Attention Step. Tell them what you like about them.

2. Remind the prospects of the Primary Interest, Dominant Buying Motive. "You said you wanted _____and_____, for this reason_____. Right?"

3. Promise them they will receive what they wanted, for the reasons they wanted it. (Satisfy the Primary Interest, which will give them the Specific Benefits they wanted, and in turn will gratify their Dominant Buying Motive.)

4. Conviction Step if necessary: Facts and Benefits, Charts, Graphs, Research, Documentation, Evidence.

5. Close.

When we return for the second step of the sale, the Presentation, we remind our prospects what they said they wanted, using their words, and the reasons they wanted that, again using their words.

Then we restate the Specific Promise, using their words as much as possible. The Specific Promise is where we promise our prospects they will receive the benefits they wanted for the reasons they wanted them. This lets them know that we are promising them *exactly* what it was they said they wanted. We want this to be fresh in their minds.

For instance, I consider my experience with a young couple interested in buying insurance. At the first meeting we could not finish the sale, because the husband had a problem to attend to. When I returned the next week to complete the sale, I told them, "First I want to make sure I have correctly recorded what you wanted. You said you are interested in insured savings so your daughter will have money for college. You want to pay for some but not all of it. You do not want term insurance, but you used to have some whole life that was too much money for you. You want to be able to put money away, but you want to be able to afford it. That way you do not have to worry about whether your daughter can afford the education you want for her. Is that about right?" They said, "Yes."

Then I restated the Specific Promise. "I have an insured savings program for you that will give money for your daughter for college. It will pay for some but not all of it. It is not term insurance, and it is not too much money, like your whole life was. You will be able to put the money away and you will be able to afford it."

Three notes: First, I did not say, "I want to remind you of what you said," but, "I want to make sure I correctly recorded what you wanted." Second, notice that the Specific Promise is almost verbatim what this couple wanted. Third, if you are interested in determining whether you should write down what the prospect wanted, try to recall this Specific Promise three days from now. I write down the information I get in the Info. Later when I make the presentation, I read the information to the prospect to make sure it is correct.

Our job is not to impress prospects with our ability to memorize, but to help them achieve what they want, for the reasons they want.

Advantages of the two-step sale

The two-step sale has some disadvantages—namely, extra time required and memory—but there are many advantages:

1. When we return to make the Presentation, we are no longer strangers. By now we are their agents. We have had a chance to sell ourselves and they like us better.

2. They are impressed with the fact that we did not try to sell them something but spent our time finding out what was important to them. They trust us more.

3. We have a chance to prepare our Presentation rather than put one together on the spot. If it is complicated, we can even practice it.

4. If we are new to the business, we can have someone else help us put the Presentation together. Then we can go back to the prospects alone and make a professional Presentation.

5. We find many of the Objections in the first step, the Info, and we can handle them before they are voiced during the second step, the Presentation.

6. Many times we determine who the decision maker is in the Info. That way we can make sure that person is present for the Close. This sometimes eliminates a Put-Off.

7. We have the opportunity to prepare the evidence we feel we will need in the Presentation.

A two-step sale is great if it fits your product and your style of selling. I happen to like a two step.

In the many forms of selling that require multi-step Presentations, it is imperative that the review of the previous step or steps be accomplished. As salespeople, we should have everything organized and reviewed when we meet again with the buyer or decision maker.

The professional salesperson will bring the buyers up to date during the second step. The professional salesperson will do so in a manner that will motivate buyers to be in a buying mood prior to the time the solutions to their problems are presented. The purpose of all the steps is to sell, not to tell.

CHAPTER 19

GETTING WARM PROSPECTS

M any people say, "I am a great salesperson if I don't have to go out and find prospects." Sorry, Charlie. Selling is a prospecting business. That is where you earn your commissions.

Others say, "You have to do the things you hate in order to get the things you like." Sorry again, Charlie. I refuse to spend the rest of my life doing things I hate. It is too easy to devise a way to make every aspect of selling more palatable, including prospecting.

There are many ways to make prospecting easier on prospect and salesperson. One way is simply to use an Attention Step and General Interest Statement when calling on the phone or in person. That will warm up the cold prospect.

Another way is to make the prospecting call enjoyable, like a party. People would rather attend a party than a business meeting. For this reason, make the phone call a happy occasion. If someone enjoys the phone call, they are more apt to meet with you. If they enjoy the phone call, they will expect to enjoy the meeting.

Play your hunches when determining which prospect to call first. When you feel like your phone call will be successful, it has more chance of being successful. When you do have success on the first call, the others will become easier and result in more success. Success breeds success.

Get Referrals

Everybody who has been in selling for any length of time knows that the best prospects come from referrals. Yet so many salespeople go through the agony of cold calling, list buying, or other forms of prospecting that are less effective. It seems that they forget to ask for referrals. Really, forgetting is not the cause of the problem. If asking for referrals were fun, they would remember to ask.

The major cause of the problem is the fear of rejection. Salespeople know they are supposed to ask for referrals and they know how to ask. They have the fear of rejection for good reason; often they are going to be rejected.

Another major reason salespeople do not ask for referrals when they should is because they feel like they are begging. The feeling is natural, because in many instances, they are begging.

The solution to the problem is not to tell them again that they should remember to ask for referrals. The solution is to show them a method where they will not encounter as much rejection and won't feel like they need a tin cup.

Most often salespeople are trained to ask for referrals on a me-oriented rather than customer-oriented basis. Some are trained to say, "You realize that I make my living by talking to people, and unless I get new names, I am out of business. Who do you know that I can talk to about my product?" That is sort of like the old ploy of, "I am working my way through college by selling magazines and I need you to help me or I will not get an education." (Do me a favor and give me the names of your friends so I can bug them.)

There is another way to ask for referrals wherein the salesperson does not come right out and say, "Do it for me," but just starts by asking if the customer could give the names of three other successful people, or maybe the names of relatives and friends. The salesperson does not tell them what the purpose is in getting those names. That is supposed to get away from the begging for a favor; but, of course, the customer knows.

If and when the customer comes up with names, the salesperson asks, "When I call these people for an appointment, may I say you gave me their names?" or, "Would you write a note telling them that they should talk to me?" Again this is salesperson-oriented rather than customer-oriented.

Painless Referrals*

In the life insurance business, when our agents finished with a client's program or made a sale, they would ask, "Do you like what I have done for you?" Obviously the answer would be, "Yes," because the clients just bought. Then the agent would say, "Thank you. Do you really mean that?" If they said, "Yes," the agent could assume that they were happy with the results of the presentation.

The purpose of the next question was to discover what aspect of the service it was that the client liked, so the question was, "What did you like most about my service?" The client would always tell what he or she liked most. It might be something like, "I liked the fact that you discovered what it was that best fit our needs rather than just trying to sell us some insurance."

The agent would again say, "Thank you. Do you really mean that?" and of course the client would say, "Yes." The next question is, "Who else do you know who might appreciate help discovering what their needs are rather than being sold some insurance?" Now the agent is doing a favor for the client's friends rather than begging for leads. It is customer-oriented rather than salesperson-oriented. It works.

---

* I borrowed the word "painless" from Denise Roberts, of D. A. Roberts & Associates, in Bloomfield Hills, Michigan, although the method I have described for getting painless referrals is not hers. She has an excellent training program entitled *Painless Prospecting* which helps salespeople eliminate much of the fear of rejection when making calls.

I asked Dave what he liked most about my service after he bought from me. He told me that it was the first time he had understood what he had in life insurance. I thanked him and asked him if he really meant that. He said, "Absolutely, this stuff has always been a mystery for me."

I asked him who else he knew that might appreciate being able to understand their insurance. Right away he said, "My dad. He has no idea of what he has." I asked Dave if he would like me to help his dad figure out what he had and he said, "Yes, he would like that."

I was not begging for a name or putting him on the spot but doing the same good thing for his father that I had done for him. When I called his dad for an appointment, his dad would look forward to meeting me. The secret was to make it pleasurable for both of them. If I could do that, then I would enjoy the process rather than fearing it.

The next question I asked Dave was, "What do you like most about your dad?" Dave told me, "He helped me change my life by showing me how to put together almost a half million dollars worth of real estate."

I asked Dave if I could tell his dad the good things he said about him. Of course, he said, "Yes." So now Dave was not only going to get the credit for sending someone to help his father solve a problem he had, but Dave would get credit for saying such good things about him. In this particular case, it was probably the first time it had ever happened.

I had another question to ask of Dave. "Do you think that your dad should meet with me, maybe have a cup of coffee?" Naturally he said, "Yes."

This is Customer-Driven Sales. Every aspect of getting the referral was to benefit the person who gave me the referral and the person I was referred to. I was not acting as a salesperson but as someone who would solve a problem for his dad.

Notice that I did not mention the word "referral." I did not mention the word "appointment." People do not want to give referrals to salespeople, and people do not want appointments with anybody. The people who are associated with appointments all hurt you or take your money.

I did not mention anything I would do for myself, only good things for them. They enjoy the process and the best part is yet to come.

The Custom-Built Attention Step

When I called Dave's dad, the first thing I said when he answered the phone was, "Mr. _____, I was talking with your son yesterday, and he said some things about you. I thought you would like to know what they were." Of course, he said, "Yes." I do not even think I told him my name. Why should I? At this point he didn't care.

After he said "Yes," I told him, "Dave said that you taught him the business so well that he has been able to put together almost a million dollars in real estate. He says that you changed his life." Then I shut up and let him tell how good that made him feel.

Then I said, "Dave also said that you should meet with me, maybe have a cup of coffee. Would you have a cup of coffee with me?" He said, "Yes." They almost always do.

Sometimes people will ask what we will be talking about. If Dave's dad did so, I would have told him that Dave said I could probably solve a problem for him, and then I would again ask, "Would you have a cup of coffee with me?"

The secret is to let them know the referrer said something about them. They will expect something bad, so when they get a great compliment, they invariably enjoy it. And I guarantee you that whatever was on their mind when you called is gone and is replaced by one of the best things that has happened all day. What an Attention Step!

This method is fun for everyone, with no stress, confrontation, or rejection. Just to make sure, when asking questions of the referrer, ask this, "Do you feel the person whose name you gave me will find it interesting meeting with me?" They will say, "Yes." Then you can tell the prospect, "Dave says you will find it interesting meeting with me. Would you have a cup of coffee with me?"

The key is that this approach is different from anything they have ever heard from salespeople before. If, in the telephone conversation, a person has an enjoyable experience, he or she will expect the face-to-face appointment to be an enjoyable experience and will meet with you more readily.

The Painless Semi-Referral

I went to see the sales manager of a television station. I did not want to make a cold call so I called Rita Burnett, a friend of mine who worked at the station. I asked Rita what she liked most about the sales manager. Rita said that she was very professional, in her dress, in her actions, and in the way she worked with the salespeople. I asked if she thought it would be interesting for the sales manager to have lunch with me. Of course, she said, "Yes."

I then asked Rita if I could tell the sales manager the good things she said about her. Rita said, "Yes." I called the sales manager on the phone and told her the nice things Rita had said about her. She enjoyed that. I then told her that Rita felt that she would find it interesting to have lunch with me. I asked her if she would, and she said, "Yes."

All three of us benefited from the phone call. The sales manager received a nice compliment, Rita got credit for the compliment, and I obtained the prospect's favorable attention and therefore the appointment.

I wanted to make a presentation to a statewide sales company with many branch offices. I did not know anyone there who could refer me to the director of training, but I did know someone who knew someone who knew him. I talked to a man who was a graduate of my sales class, finding out what he knew about a woman in management with this sales company.

I called her and told her about the nice things this man had said about her. Then I met with her over a cup of coffee. I told her about the type of training I did, and that I was going to call the director of training for an appointment. I then asked her what she liked about him. She told me some nice things about him and gave me permission to tell him what she had said.

I called the director of training and told him that this woman who worked with him had told me some things about him that I thought he would like to hear. Of course, he said, "Yes." I told him of the compliments she had paid him and let him say how much he appreciated it. Then I told him that she had suggested that he would find having lunch with me interesting, and I asked him if he would. He agreed.

He knew I was a sales trainer, and on the way to lunch, he told me that his company was happy with the five national training companies they worked with. Still he met with me because of my Attention Step. He did find the lunch interesting, because I asked the right questions and found a problem the company had that I could solve. I ended up with the biggest sale I had ever made.

The interesting part of this experience was that there really was no referral to the prospect. I merely asked the woman to tell me the things she liked about someone that I was going to approach and asked her if she felt it might be interesting for him to have lunch with me. There was no reluctance on her part and no fear of rejection on mine.

In this situation an ordinary approach would have been doomed for failure. By using the third-party compliment, I made it difficult for him to turn me down for lunch. It was easy, it was fun, it was a great experience for everyone concerned. The organization ended up better than it had been before, and so did I.

In using this type of warm calling, salespeople find that they don't forget to get referrals, they don't dread phoning for appointments, and they don't have to worry where they are going to get the money to buy the lunch.

There is no reason to make a cold call. When calling on a company where I know no one, I find someone who knows the person I want to see or one of that person's superiors. If I start out with the person's superior, I am in the enviable position of being sent to the prospect by the boss.

I do not ask for a referral. I ask what he or she likes about the management person I will call on. When the prospect is a man, I say, "I am going to be making a call on him. May I tell him the nice things you said about him?" The person will invariably say, "Yes." The same with women, except that I use the pronoun her. When I ask if the person feels the prospect will enjoy talking with me, he or she always says, "Yes."

This method of getting referrals or new prospects is nonthreatening and leads to an approach that is less threatening. The person who gives the referral helps build the Attention Step that makes it easier to get appointments. Just do not call them appointments; remember, people who make appointments hurt you and take your money.

CHAPTER 20

THE EASIEST SALE YOU WILL EVER MAKE

A lmost every time I put gas in my car, I use the same service station. I go to the same cleaners year after year. The same with buying tires; I always go to Brogan's. If I need information on casualty insurance, I call Dave Havrilla. It is the same with everything I buy. This is true with other people also. The terminology "Patronage Buying Motive" means going to the place or person you patronized before and doing business there again and again.

People do not even check anybody else's service or prices as long as we maintain a relationship with them. We practically have to drive customers away in order for them to consider going to somebody else. How many times have you known you could do better than the competitor who has the account and heard, "We are happy with our present supplier"? How many times have you heard, "My uncle is in the business"? The relationship maintains the business.

Maintain a Relationship

Once we build a relationship we must maintain it or watch it disappear. Lisa was married to Bruce. Bruce's brother, Rich, is an investment adviser. Lisa used to do her investing through Rich. Lisa got a divorce from Bruce. Lisa has a new investment adviser. The relationship disappeared, and the business disappeared along with it.

A salesperson had convinced me that her hotel was the best place to hold my classes on Customer-Driven Sales. The hotel was in the right location, the room was the right size, and the price was competitive. The staff took great care to set the room up exactly as I wanted, so there was no reason to go anywhere else. Yet I left there after one class. Here's why.

A few weeks after I signed the contract, I became less important to them. Several times we were moved to a different room without notice; I had to call for coffee twice; and they would set the room up differently than it was supposed to be. Our honeymoon was over.

All the hotel personnel had to do was keep the original relationship going. The salesperson had been promoted and left. Had she stayed she would have made things right. I know that. I also know that there were a couple of other people in the same department who could have done the same thing. I did not want anything special, just to have them look after my needs, stroke me, and let me know that I was important to them. I just wanted service after the sale.

When we have made a sale, all of a sudden we are no longer a supplier; we are *their* supplier. Once customers buy real estate, insurance, or investments from an agent, that person becomes *their* agent. Once we are in that position, when we have that relationship, it is simple to continue to be their supplier, their agent, or their salesperson.

Keep those cards and letters coming

After the sale there are many ways to maintain a successful continuing relationship. For example, follow up on the sale with a note; not a note of thanks for the business, but a note telling how much you enjoyed meeting them and working with them. My mother said, "When someone has invited you to dinner and you send them a thank-you note, don't thank them for the meal, tell them how much you enjoyed their company." In Customer-Driven Sales the key is the relationship that exists between the parties, not the money that changes hands. Relish the money, but to keep it coming, maintain the relationship.

Life insurance agents seem to have a monopoly on sending birthday cards, partially because in the conduct of their business they learn the birthdays of their clients. Another reason is that people believe that a good time to buy more insurance is just before you turn a year older.

When I receive a birthday card with a preprinted phrase, I throw it away. If I get a handwritten note along with it, I keep it. Most people appreciate the personal touch, rather than a card the secretary sends out automatically.

When I was in the life insurance business I made a point of sending birthday cards to my clients' children. I would write in the style of the age of the child. For a three year old, I would print, "Happy Birthday," left-handed in a childish scrawl. As they grew older my handwriting would improve along with the way I thought they would write. Those cards ended up in the hands of the children rather than being thrown away, and the children knew who I was.

Let them know they are special

Lynne Van Deventer does so many things right in selling residential real estate. Once I went with her to see a home she was going to show. As it was not her listing, she had not been in the house. She met the woman who would be there when the house was to be shown and met her children, learning their names and talking to them at their level.

Many real estate agents are strictly business when talking to home owners prior to showing their homes. Lynne was very warm. She complimented the cleanliness of the home, and listened when the woman told how much she had enjoyed living there. Many agents tell home owners that they have to be out of the home while it is being shown. Lynne does not tell home owners what they have to do. She suggested that the owner remain in the yard in case there were any questions she could answer to assist in the sale.

In every way Lynne treated the woman and her family like very special people. She treated them like customers should be treated, even though they were not her customers. I believe that particular house sold without being listed again with another agent. If the listing had run out before the home was sold, who do you think would get the call to list it?

There are people in business who are together more than many families; they spend eight to twelve hours per day together. It is best to treat everyone in the business as a valued customer so everyone knows you really are nice.

Betty Jane Minsky had her favorite refrigeration repairman to the house because her freezer stopped working. He told her that the necessary part would not be in until the next day, so she should keep the door closed so the contents would not thaw. Betty Jane told him she would be gone but would leave the key so he could get in the house to fix it.

When she came home the next day she found the sink full of bags of blueberries that had thawed out because the freezer had not been fixed. There was a note on the sink that said, "The part did not arrive, so I came out to the house to take anything out of the freezer that would thaw and leak on everything else."

Betty Jane told me she was happy with the repair service even though they had not been able to fix the freezer that day. What they had done was more important to her; they made a special trip to the house to make sure she did not suffer the consequences of the proper part not arriving in time. This is an example of how to maintain the relationship through customer service even when the product service is not performed.

Building the Warm Relationship

Another way to maintain the relationship is to be enthusiastic in your greeting when you see your clients in settings other than a business situation. Don't greet them with a quiet, "Hi," but with an enthusiastic, *"Hiiii!"* like you are really glad to see them. Do that with excitement, and they will know you are really glad to see them, not sell them. You sell yourself, and you sell your product. If you keep selling them on yourself and strengthening your relationship, you will keep selling them your product.

Stop in when you are in the neighborhood but don't stay too long. Well-trained restaurant servers do this, checking to see if there is anything their customers need, making themselves visible without being a bother. Once when I called a client on business, he said, "You only call me when you want money." I decided this would not happen again.

It did happen again. I contacted one of my better clients whom I had forgotten about for a couple of years and found that he had bought from someone else. The problem was that while I had decided it would not happen again, I had not become organized to make sure it would not happen again.

After I finished talking to a food processors' convention, a member of the audience came up and asked if it was a good idea to stop and see customers when he had nothing to sell them. I told him, "Yes, if you do not stay too long." Later on, he wrote me a letter stating that he had done so a couple of times and received a warm greeting each time. He told of another benefit he received from the visits. When he came out after the brief encounter, he had renewed enthusiasm to carry with him to his next appointment. He also picked up a couple of sales that he may have missed if he had not stopped just to say, "Hello."

Stopping unannounced is to be used with care. Make sure you do not make it a habit and become a bother. The situation with a purchasing manager is different than it would be with a store manager or an entrepreneur. Most people appreciate knowing that every once in a while someone will stop to see them without trying to sell them something. Of course, sometimes when the relationship call is made, a manager will say, "I'm glad you just stopped in, I was thinking of calling you."

When you read something complimentary about clients or their companies in periodicals, send them a copy with a personal note. When you read something that you feel would be important to you if you were in that person's job, send a copy of that. Every once in a while I receive a newspaper copy that refers to me. I generally appreciate that. Every once in a while I receive newspaper copy that refers to what somebody sells to me. I generally throw that away.

When in a selling situation, ask questions to make sure that what you are selling is something that will benefit the prospect. Be a good listener and encourage others to talk about themselves. In other words, sell on a customer-driven basis. Talk in terms of their interests. Help them solve their problems, accomplish their goals, and make their dreams come true. This is one of the best ways to build lasting relationships.

A Reminder to Do What You Already Know How to Do

The information in this chapter is not new, and you probably have heard it before. In fact, a great source of material on building relationships was published in 1936: *How to Win Friends and Influence People,* by Dale Carnegie. Read the book. It is a great reminder.

The easiest sale you will ever make is the one you already made. Once you have turned prospects into customers, it is easy to keep them as customers if you show them you are interested in them. Your competition will have to work extra hard to take them away if you do what you are supposed to do. If you do not do what you are supposed to do, you will make it easy for competitors to sneak in and take them over.

Julie Goff sold advertising for a community newspaper. One of her customers was five weeks behind in paying for her ads, so Julie went to see her. Julie told the woman that the account was five weeks behind in payment, but the client thought it amounted to four weeks. In fact she had a check for that amount ready for Julie.

They discussed the difference and the woman insisted she owed for only four weeks. Julie said, "Whatever you feel is right is OK." The woman said she knew it was four weeks, so Julie accepted that amount as payment in full.

Some people at the newspaper may have insisted that the woman pay for the extra week, but the result would be losing a customer. Julie kept a customer who will buy week after week and will spend many times more than the small amount that was forgiven. Do not be afraid to let the customer win in a small disagreement. You will win the customer.

Colleen O'Donnell says to break bread with clients. An Irish tradition says that if you break bread together, you form a bond. That same bonding takes place today when you have lunch with someone who is already your customer.

After you have done everything right with your customers, their children, their business associates, and everyone else you can think of, you make the big sale. But remember, you may have made the sale, but someone else can lose it for you. So check the letters that go to your customers to make sure they say what you would like them to say. Many times letters sent to your customers may be written by those who have no knowledge of proper human relations. Sometimes letters sent out by companies contain phrases that you would not send to your enemies.

For example, my office lease required that I pay the rent by the fifth of the month. After having been there for two years and having always paid my rent on the first of the month, I received a letter from my friend, the manager of the building. It was a reminder that the rent was due on or before the fifth of the month, and a warning that if I did not pay by that time, it would be considered overdue. It was signed by my friend.

Obviously the letter was directed to some renters who did not pay their rent on time, but everyone in the building received the same letter. A letter such as that should not have gone to anyone, including those who were guilty of paying late.

Take good care of the customers you already have, and make sure others in the company do so too. Do not forget your present customers. Continue building relationships, and as a result you will end up with some of the easiest sales you will ever make, simply by keeping those you already have.

CHAPTER 21

AN EXCEPTION TO POSITIVE MENTAL ATTITUDE

All of the top salespeople in the world will say that having a positive attitude has contributed to their success. Every motivational speaker who has ever talked to salespeople says the same thing: "If you want to be more successful, have a positive attitude." Every writer who has given advice on the subject has stated that one of the keys to success in selling is having a positive attitude.

There is probably nobody in the whole wide world who would disagree with that tidbit of information. Every salesperson who has spent any time in the business has heard it at least a hundred times. "If you wish to be successful in sales, develop a positive attitude." It is so popular that it is even recognized by its own set of initials, PMA.

I agree with the experts; no matter what we do for a living, we will be more successful if we have a positive mental attitude. Everyone knows if we are positive or negative because, whether we realize it or not, we radiate our attitude. It has been said that we wear our attitude on the back of our heads, where everyone else can see it but we cannot.

The opposite of having a positive mental attitude is being negative. There is no situation I know of where a negative attitude will enhance sales performance. There is, however, one time when we can enhance sales performance by consciously eliminating both the positive and the negative thoughts about making a sale.

Forget the "Winning Attitude"

Some experts say that when we approach a sales presentation, we should have a winning attitude that we are going to close the sale. For the real heavy hitters this may be apropos, if that is what they wish. For the majority of sales people, it is self-defeating. And it has no place in Customer-Driven Sales.

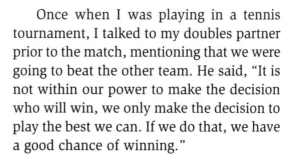

Once when I was playing in a tennis tournament, I talked to my doubles partner prior to the match, mentioning that we were going to beat the other team. He said, "It is not within our power to make the decision who will win, we only make the decision to play the best we can. If we do that, we have a good chance of winning."

I should have known that. We have no control over who will win a game, but we do have control over how we play the game. Many times I have concentrated on winning when I should have expended my efforts doing what I was supposed to do. If I had concentrated on doing what I was supposed to do, I would have had a better chance of winning.

When I was a new agent with Northwestern Mutual Life Insurance Company, we had a monthly sales-builder meeting which was presided over by the general agent, Byron Crosse. We reported on our activity and sales for the previous month. Then we projected what we would sell the next month, along with the activity we felt we needed to accomplish that projection.

Byron never faulted us for not hitting the sales goal, but he did get upset when we did not hit our activity goals. His point was that we had set the activity goals we wanted, and that it was within our ability to attain them. We could not control the results, but we could control the activity required to obtain those results.

In selling, we have the ability to control how many phone calls we make and the number of presentations we make, but not the results of the calls or presentations. Many times results are based on variables and circumstances beyond our control.

If prior to making a call, I tell myself that I am going to make a sale, I am setting myself up for rejection. If I do not make the sale, I have experienced failure, and my subconscious realizes that I did not do what I said I was going to do. That will make the next call more difficult.

Success breeds success, but failure breeds failure. I have the ability to eliminate that failure.

Instead of thoughts that will cause fear of failure or result in possible rejection, I tell myself prior to making a call that I will concentrate on doing the things that will bring success. Then I can experience success, regardless of whether I make the sale or not. I have no control over the sale, only over what I do to make the sale.

I used to wonder, "What if I do all the things that are required to become successful, and I don't make it in this business?" But generally, when I did all the things I was supposed to do, I was successful.

L. Gray Burdin, who was Director of Instruction for the Dale Carnegie Course, was quoted by Dick Morgul, one of the Instructor Trainers, as saying, "When you are less concerned about where you are going, and more concerned about what you do to get there, you will get where you want to go."

Try the Problem-Solving Attitude

In Customer-Driven Sales our job is to solve our prospects' problems with our products and services. This means we should have that purpose in mind when we approach them. Doing so will reduce the fear of rejection and enhance the image we have of ourselves in being customer-oriented rather than product-oriented. Another advantage is that when we approach prospects to solve their problems, they will realize that we have their best interests in mind.

Approaching prospects with the idea of seeing if they have a problem we can solve does not mean that we drop our positive attitude. It means only that we change our thoughts while making the approach from, "I am going to make a sale here," to, "I am going to see if this person or business has a problem I can solve." The positive attitude is still there, intact and operating.

This is similar to the purpose a doctor may have on approaching the examination of a patient. The purpose of the exam is to determine if the patient has a problem the doctor can solve, not to sell the patient on having surgery.

How would you like to go to a doctor, dentist, attorney, or other professional when you knew the purpose of the interview was to sell you something? Salespeople are professionals also.

If It Is to Be, It Is Up to Me

To a certain extent, attitude is not a matter of choice. You cannot just decide that you are going to change your attitude for the better and have it happen, anymore than you can just decide that you are going to pick up a saxophone and play it. You might decide that, but it is not going to happen. What we all can do, however, is decide to work at changing our attitude. Like the ten two-letter words at the beginning of this paragraph, *If it is to be, it is up to me.*

In this particular case, where we only wish to change our attitude going into a sale, it is easy to accomplish.

If you feel you are a victim of circumstances and there is nothing you can do about it, you are obviously negative. Even if this is true, you are OK if only you will try. You do not have to believe you can improve to do so; all you have to do is work at it.

Chapter 21   An Exception to Positive Mental Attitude

We all have single-track minds. We cannot think of two different things at once. In order to determine what our attitude should be while making an approach, all we have to do is decide what will be the purpose of the meeting. If we decide that the purpose of the meeting is to sell the prospect something, that is what will be on our minds. If we decide to learn whether the prospect has a problem we can solve, that is what will be on our minds. We make the decision. Generally we can sense the attitude in others who sell to us, so I suspect they can sense ours also.

We are not changing our overall attitude on selling—only the attitude we have going into the sales presentation. It is easy to do if that truly is our purpose. If it really is not our purpose, we are lying to ourselves. I am sure that is not the case for you, however, because otherwise you would not be reading a book on how to make the change to Customer-Driven Sales.

Appendix 1

TRACK THEORY

- Attention Step
- Indicator (Optional)
- General Interest Statement
- Bridge to Info

- Info: Fact-Finding Questions

  Standard Feeling-Finding Questions

  Menu

  (Determine Primary Interest, Specific Benefits, and

  Dominant Buying Motive)

- Specific Promise

  Trial Close

  If required—Conviction Step (Facts and Benefits)

  Trial Close

  Evidence (If required)

  Trial Close

  Handle Objections

  Trial Close

- Close

Appendix 2

TRACK WORDS

The following is a sample of how the Track Theory can be put into practice:

- **Attention:** I compliment you on taking the time to improve your selling with an emphasis on Customer-Driven Sales. *Thank you.*

- **Indicator:** The fact that you are reading this book would indicate that you are the type of person who would also be interested in other ways of improving your sales. Would that be correct? *Yes.*

- **General Interest Statement:** The reason I mention that, is because we have a program here in your city designed to help salespeople much like you, who are interested in making the change to Customer-Driven Sales, to improve even more, become more professional, and possibly prepare for advancement. I feel we could help you do the same.

- **Bridge to Info:** In order to determine how much benefit you can receive, and to conserve your time, may I ask you some questions? *Sure.*

Fact-Finding Questions:

What do you sell?
I sell space for the local television station.

How long have you been there?
About six months now.

Do you like it?
I love it.

What did you do before you started selling television space?
I sold radio for a couple of years here in town.

Are you on commission, salary, or salary plus commission?
I am on straight commission. It's the only way to go.

Have you ever taken a class in selling before?
Yes, I took a two-week sales class put on by my radio station.

- **Feeling-Finding Questions:**

What did you like most about the class you took?
I liked the fact that I found out that selling could be learned. I learned quite a bit.

Why was that important to you?
I had always used the trial-and-error method before and was not doing too well. The class made me money.

What did you dislike most about that class?
So much of the training was canned presentation where we did all the talking.

Why was that a problem for you?
I don't like it when salespeople try to sell me something without listening to what I want, and I can't see doing it to somebody else. It's not professional.

If I could do something differently in helping you become more professional, what would you want that to be?
I want to learn how to ask questions in an organized manner rather than probing for information.

Why would that be important to you?

I would be able to talk about what my prospects are interested in rather than having to guess. So many times I am telling them what they don't want to hear about, because I have not done a good job in information gathering.

- **Menu:**

  Many salespeople like you, who are interested in doing a better job in their information gathering, take the Customer-Driven Sales class. There are different reasons salespeople like the program:

  - One of the reasons is that they gain even *more confidence* in selling; not "I can," or "I will," but the kind of confidence that comes when they *know* they are good. This added confidence is transmitted to their prospects and helps increase sales.

  - Others like the Selling Skills; they learn how to get prospects to want to hear about what they are selling, how to handle objections, and how to close more effectively. This is where they develop the basics of selling and put those basics into practice.

  - Some salespeople find out how to do a better job of Motivating People to buy now. By doing so, they eliminate some of the no's and put-offs and get less rejections and more sales. If prospects do not buy now, they may never buy, or they may buy from someone else later.

  - And then there are those who like the fact that they learn more about Customer-Driven Sales. They are able to get their prospects to give them the information they need to solve problems, rather than just sell a product. This way the salespeople know how to talk in terms of the customer's needs. The result: long-term customers rather than a quick sale.

Mr. Prospect, of these major benefits, developing even More Confidence in selling, putting the Selling Skills into practice, doing a better job Motivating People, or learning more about Customer-Driven Sales, which do you feel would be most important to you?
Customer-Driven Sales. **(PI)**

Why did you choose that one?
Like I said before, I want to be able to talk about what they are interested in rather than just guessing what will turn them on. **(Specific Benefit)**

Mr. Prospect, assume that I could help you do a better job of organizing your questioning so you could talk about what your clients are interested in, why would that be important to you?
I would feel more professional. **(Specific Benefit)**

You mentioned that before, feeling more professional. Why would that be so important to you?
The way I was raised was to do everything first rate. There was never any room for being "just good" at something. **(DBM)**

- **Specific Promise:**

  Mr. Prospect, you go through this class, and you will learn how to ask questions in an organized manner rather than probing or guessing. That way you will be able to talk about what prospects are interested in. This will help you feel more professional. After all, like you say, there is no room for being just good.

- **Trial Close:** How does that sound?
  It sounds like just what I want.

- **Trial Close:** Would that be worth 30 hours of your time?
  Yes.

- **Trial Close:** Would that be worth an investment of $____?
  You bet.

- **Close:** Please put your name on this form, the way you want it to appear on your records.

Appendix 3

RULE SHEETS

On the following pages are tear-out Rule Sheets for each chapter, starting with Chapter 2. Each sheet serves as a reminder for you to use the rule covered in that chapter. Here is how the sheets can be used to incorporate the rules into your selling:

1. Fill in the blank spaces on each card, using your own words to incorporate the rule.

2. Put the completed Rule Sheet where it will be highly visible to you. Some people put it on the sun-visor or dash of the car. Others put it in the front of their appointment book.

3. Read the sheet and practice the rule prior to meeting with a prospect. Critique yourself after the presentation.

4. Determine what approaches fit your style best. Either decide to use the sheet the same way at the next presentation or to change it.

5. Save each sheet as you edit it. When you complete all of them, staple them together. Take a good look at the finished product. That is probably the way you should be selling.

Chapter 2

Attention Reminder

Before I make a presentation, I will get my prospect to focus on me and to like me.

I will concentrate on the following attention getters:

1. _____

_____

_____

_____

2. _____

_____

_____

_____

3. _____

_____

_____

_____

Optional Chapter 3

Attention Step, Indicator, and General Interest

At the beginning of my presentation, I will pay my prospects a compliment and tell them what it indicates to me:

This indicates to me _____

_____.

Would that be correct?

The Prospect will say, "Yes."

The reason I mention that is because (I have) (we have) _____

_____

_____

and I feel (I) (we) can do the same for you.

Chapter 4

General Interest Statement with Bridge to Info

Before gathering information from a prospect, I will arouse interest with a General Interest Statement and Bridge to Info.

(I) (We) have helped many other _____,

much like you, to _____

_____,

_____ and

_____,

and (I) (we) feel (I) (we) can do the same for you.

Bridge to Info: In order to determine how much benefit you can receive, and to conserve your time, may I ask you some questions?

Chapter 5
Feeling-Finding Questions

After asking Fact-Finding Questions, I will ask my prospects the following Feeling-Finding Questions:

- What do you like most about (present, past, other products)?

  _____

- Why is that important to you? _____

- What do you dislike most about (present, past, other products)?

  _____

- Why is that a problem for you? _____

- If I were to (do this), (furnish your next one), what would you want me to do differently? _____

- Why would that be important to you? _____

(Now I may have found the Primary Interest. If not, I should go to the Menu.)

Chapter 6

Determining the Primary Interest

- In order to know what aspect of my product to talk about, I must determine what primarily interests my prospects.

- After I determine their Primary Interest, I must then find out what Specific Benefits they would like to receive by having the Primary Interest satisfied.

- Many times the Primary Interest can be determined simply by asking the Standard Feeling-Finding questions. Sometimes prospects will tell me without being asked any questions. There are also times when I must use a Menu to make the determination.

One way or another, I need to get this information.

Chapter 7

Determining the Specific Benefits

I need to determine the Specific Benefits my prospects want to gain as a result of achieving their Primary Interest. In order to do this, after finding their Primary Interest, I will ask the following questions:

- If you could do that, why would that be important to you?

- How would that benefit you?

- What would that do for you?

I will continue asking these questions until I understand specifically how they expect to benefit from owning my product.

Chapter 8

Determining the Dominant Buying Motive

I need to determine what will move my prospects to make the decision to buy. In order to do so, I must determine the Dominant Buying Motive. To do this I ask these questions:

- How would that benefit **you**?

- What would that do for **you**?

- Why would that be important to **you**?

In asking these questions, the emphasis is placed on the word **you**, because I want to determine what feeling or emotional benefit the buyer will achieve. I will only ask the number of questions required to get the answer I want.

Chapter 9

Specific Promise

After I determine a prospect's Primary Interest, Specific Benefits, and Dominant Buying Motive, I will promise to deliver them to the prospect. (Only promise what I can accomplish.)

I can do that. I can give you (the Primary Interest you want)
or
You (buy this product) (use our service) (let me _____
your_____) and you will (attain the Primary Interest
you want).

Which means you will obtain the (Specific Benefits you wanted), so you can (satisfy your Dominant Buying Motive).

Trial Close: _____?

Chapter 10

Finding the Primary Interest by Menu

One of the reasons people like my _____

is because they _____.

Others say they _____.

Some find that they _____,

and there are others that like _____.

Of these major benefits, _____,

_____, _____,

and _____, which would be most important to you?

Determine the Specific Benefits and Dominant Buying Motive:

- Why did you choose that one?

- How would that benefit you?

- What would that do for you?

Chapter 11
Create Your Own Menu

_____ , _____

_____

_____

_____

_____ , _____

_____

_____

_____

_____ , _____

_____

_____

_____

_____ , _____

_____

_____

_____

_____ , _____

_____

Chapter 12

Feel, Felt, Found (with no buts)

Before I answer an Objection, I will first use a cushion:

- I understand how you feel.

- I know what you mean.

Then I will let them know they are not alone:

- I felt the same way, or about the same way.

- (Name)_____ felt the same way.

- Others have felt the same way.

Then I will tie a Benefit to it:

- Here is what I found: _____.

- Here is what (he) (she) found: _____.

- Here is what they found _____.

[Give a Benefit that solves the problem or offsets it.]

If the Objection cannot be answered or solved, cushion it and let them know they are not alone.

Trial Close: _____?

Chapter 13

Weighing Close

(Name) _____, this is a pretty important decision for (you) (you and _____). In all fairness to you and _____, let's take a look at the ideas that might cause you to hesitate, and weigh them against the important reasons to go ahead with this program, and do so now:

Draw the letter "T."

First, the ideas that might cause you to hesitate:

1. You said that _____. Right? (Write it down.)

2. You also mentioned that _____. Right? (Write it down.)

Is there anything else that might cause you to hesitate?
(Write it down and ask again until there are no more reasons to hesitate.)

Now, let's take a look at the important reasons to go ahead with this _____, and do so right now:

(List how it will accomplish their Primary Interests.
List how it will accomplish their Specific Benefits.
List how it will accomplish their Dominant Buying Motive.)

Now, (name) _____, which side seems to (weigh the heavier?) (be more important to you)? (Let them answer.)

Don't you think it would be a good idea to start right now?

Chapter 14

Facts and Benefits

Each time I give a Fact about my product, I will follow it with a Benefit that the prospect indicated was important.

Each time a prospect asks a question about my product, I will answer the question and tie a Benefit to the answer.

(Answer) _____, which means you

(Benefit) _____.

The Benefit should refer to the Primary Interest, a Specific Benefit, or the Dominant Buying Motive of the prospect, or even better, to all three of them.

Chapter 15

Evidence

Demonstrations or exhibits I might use: _____

_____

Testimonials I can use: _____

_____

Examples of satisfied customers: _____

_____

Statistics I will carry with me: _____

_____

What aspects of my product will probably require evidence?

_____

_____

_____

Chapter 16

Buying Signals and Trial Closes

I will watch and listen for buying signals.

I will use Trial Closes to see if my prospect is ready to buy.

Buying signals I am likely to encounter in my selling:

- Verbal:_____

_____

_____

- Nonverbal:_____

_____

_____

- Trial Closes I can use:_____

_____

_____

_____

_____

_____

Chapter 17

The Close

When I feel the prospect is ready to buy, I will use an Assumed Close. Here are some I can use:

- Instructional:_____

_____

- Alternate:_____

_____

- Minor Point:_____

_____

After I ask, I will wait quietly until I get an answer.

Chapter 18

Two-Step Sale

If I use a two-step sale, I will develop an information gathering form to include the following questions:

- Did you ever own a product like this before?

- What did you like most about it?

- Why was that important to you?

- What did you dislike most about it?

- Why was that a problem for you?

- If I could do something different for you than you had in your last product, what would you want that to be?

- Why would that be important to you?

Possible Primary Interests I could use in the Menu:_____

_____, _____

and _____.

Chapter 19A

Painless Referral Track

What do you like most about my service? (Answer)

Thank you. Do you really mean that? (Yes)

Who else do you know who may want (restate benefit)? (Answer)

What do you like most about (that person)? Could I tell (that person) the good things you said about (him) (her)? (Yes)

Do you feel (that person) should meet with me, perhaps to have a cup of coffee? (Yes)

Thank you, I will let you know what happens.

I will write a note of thanks to those who give me names of others I can help, but I will not call them referrals.

Chapter 19B

Painless Referral Attention Step

Hi, (prospect)_____. My name is (name) _____.

I was talking with (referrer) _____ yesterday, and (he) (she) said something about you. I thought you would like to know what it was. (Yes)

(Referrer) _____ said (pay the specific compliment) _____. (Let them thank you or talk about it.)

(Referrer) _____ also said you should (have a cup of coffee) (have lunch) (meet) with me.

If they say yes, set an appointment.

If they stall or ask why: (Referrer) _____ felt I could be of benefit to you. I promise you will have an interesting time. Would you meet with me over a cup of coffee?

Chapter 20

Keeping the Easiest Sale Warm

Things I can do to build a warm relationship with my customers:

_____

_____

_____

_____

_____

_____

How I expect to benefit from following these simple rules:

_____

_____

_____

_____

_____

_____

Chapter 21

Developing a Problem-Solving Attitude

I will learn this rule verbatum and repeat it to myself prior to making a call on a prospect:

_____

_____

_____

_____

_____

_____

_____

_____

_____

_____ .

About the Author

Phil Kline is a graduate of Michigan State University, School of Business and Public Service. He was an instructor of the Dale Carnegie course for 15 years, and taught at Lansing Community College for ten years.

Phil was a member of the National Speakers Association, Professional Speakers of Michigan, American Society for Training and Development, American Marketing Association, and Sales and Marketing Executives International. He is currently a freelance writer for sales and training magazines.